P.E.N. American Center:

A History of the First Fifty Years

by Marchette Chute

P.E.N. American Center
New York City
1972

The Sean O'Casey letter on page 26 is printed
by permission of St. Martin's Press, Inc., Macmillan & Co., Ltd.,
the Frederic Melcher letter on page 49 by permission of Daniel Melcher,
and the John Steinbeck letter on page 63
by permission of McIntosh and Otis, Inc., as agents for the Steinbeck estate.

This history was made possible
through the generous support of the Ford Foundation
and of the National Endowment for the Arts in Washington, D.C.,
a Federal agency created by Act of Congress in 1965.

The writing of this history is a gift to P.E.N. from the author.

P.E.N. American Center
156 Fifth Avenue, New York City 10010

Design & typesetting: Congrat-Butlar

Printed in the United States of America

P.E.N.
American Center

Contents

INTRODUCTION   *vii*

PART ONE   **3**

PART TWO   **29**

PART THREE   **51**

PART FOUR   **73**

APPENDIX

    List of Presidents of the American Center   **107**

    List of International P.E.N. Congresses   **109**

    Text of P.E.N. Charter   **110**

INDEX   **111**

Introduction

This is the story of the American Center of the P.E.N. with head-quarters in New York City. There are now some eighty of these P.E.N. Centers all around the world, existing on a framework whose headquarters is in London. Each Center has its separate history, its triumphs and failures, its periods of stagnation or defeat and its special moments of glorious energy. This is the story of one such Center and of what has happened to it in the first half-century of its existence.

Most of the work of the American Center is done by volunteers. Officers, members of the Board, heads of committees, members of committees, workers on special projects—all these have served P.E.N., sometimes at great personal inconvenience, because they believed in the organization and valued it. In so brief a history, it has not been possible to single out more than a fraction of these people; in fact, half the Presidents are not mentioned by name, although a list of them and their terms of service will be found in the Appendix.

It is the unidentified, indispensable volunteers of P.E.N., the ones whose names do not appear in the text, to whom this history is dedicated.

M.C.

A
History
of the
First Fifty Years

Part One

On a winter day in 1881, Walt Whitman wrote a letter to a translator in Dresden in which he said: "My dearest dream is for an internationality of poems and poets, binding the lands of the earth closer than all treaties and diplomacy. . . . The purpose beneath the rest in my book is such hearty comradeship, for individuals to begin with, and for all the nations of the earth as a result."

Many writers over the years have had this dream, but it was left to a Cornish novelist and poet to do something about it. She was a short, stout woman with bright blue eyes whose name was Mrs. C. A. Dawson Scott, and she had an unshakable conviction that if the writers of the world could learn to stretch out their hands to each other, the nations of the world could learn in time to do the same. This was in 1921, in the period of bitter hatred between nations that followed the First World War.

Mrs. Dawson Scott had no special standing in the world of letters, but she turned to John Galsworthy, who did. Together they set about building an international organization of writers whose basis would be comradeship in the precise sense that Walt Whitman used the word.

They were an oddly matched pair, but they worked together superbly. Galsworthy never forgot who was the originator—"mother and nurse of the scheme"—and he would have been content with no credit at all for himself as long as the idea flourished. He was willing to spend long hours attending committee meetings, addressing envelopes, folding circulars and going through the endless details of organization so that the little seedling could be kept alive and have a chance to grow. As she said of him after they had worked together for a year: "He is a wise man, social and genial and a builder. He has laid good foundations and we work together curiously well."

It was decided to call the organization "The P.E.N. Club." The letters stood for poets, playwrights, editors, essayists and novelists, and the acronym formed an easily remembered pun.

Galsworthy immediately started rounding up every writer he could reach, and nearly every well-known man and woman of letters in England finally joined. Writers as various as Conrad and Chesterton, John Masefield and Arnold Bennett, were among the early members. Shaw resisted for three years and then wrote in capitulation: "Very well, I will go quietly. . . . After my first lunch at the Savile Club in 1876 or thereabouts, I swore I would avoid literary circles as plague areas. . . . It is on the international basis . . . that I succumb to your decree of Compulsory Service."

The P.E.N. had its first meeting in October of 1921. A dinner was held in London at the Florence Restaurant in Rupert Street and, as Galsworthy said afterwards, "To my astonishment I found myself occupying the chair." He was a shy and reserved man, by temperament not fond of social gatherings, and it was a mark of his devotion to the principle behind P.E.N. that he remained its presiding officer for the rest of his life. If he had been given a choice between the task of folding circulars and of presiding over a glittering palace ceremony in Central Europe, he would almost certainly have chosen the former; but he did both, since both would strengthen the organization. As Myra Hess said of him, "His was a universal mind," and he found in the P.E.N. a way of turning his dream into a reality. Each new member delighted him, and one of the early joiners remembered how Galsworthy had gazed at him "in a fatherly way as if pleased by another addition to his family."

It was the intention from the beginning to try to establish a P.E.N. Center in every country in the world, so that there could be a continual interchange of friendship, and it was for this reason that D. H. Lawrence, who was certainly no joiner, gave P.E.N. his affection. "Even if I'm the black sheep amongst its members, yet I feel that wherever I go P.E.N. would accept me and be kind to me if I'd let them—all over the face of the earth—which is somehow comforting."

A French Center was formed six months after the October dinner in Rupert Street, and Anatole France was its first President. Its first meeting was held in the early spring, and in this same month of March, 1922, a prospectus was mailed out in New York to announce plans for an American Center.

In the case of the American Center, Galsworthy and Mrs. Dawson Scott had done something very unusual for them: they had crossed wires. Mrs. Dawson Scott had asked Kate Douglas Wiggin, a popular American writer of the day, to gather her friends around her and organize a Center in New York. Galsworthy, on the other hand, has asked Joseph Anthony, a young American writer who was currently head of the London office of the Century Company, to act as "a committee of one . . . to get a New York branch started."

In January of 1922, Anthony wrote to "Alexander Black, novelist, and Maxwell Aley, editor," giving an outline of the plan, and Black and Aley met with a few key people in Aley's house in New York on 24th Street. Mrs. Wiggin, who had not been invited, naturally felt that she and her own group had a priority, and "a great deal of diplomacy and tact had to be exercised to harmonize the two."

By March of 1922, the Committee on Organization was in full swing. Black was its hardworking chairman and Aley its secretary, using the Century Company as the mailing address. Kate Douglas Wiggin was, of course, a member of this committee, and the other woman on it was Willa Cather, thus neatly illustrating the wide range of writers and of writing styles that the American Center has always managed to house cheerfully under one roof. The remaining members of the Committee on Organization were Carl Van Doren, Jesse Lynch Williams and a red-haired young poet named John Farrar who was editor of *The Bookman*. Farrar was frankly fascinated by the project. "This seems to us," he remarked editorially, "one of the most promising clubs to which we have ever belonged."

What the Committee lacked was a single powerful literary figure, like Galsworthy, who could persuade well-known writers to join on the basis of personal friendship and esteem. On its surface, the American Center had very little to offer except a series of dinners and an idea. Still, the idea was a good one, even if it had not yet been tested, and in a relatively short time the membership included writers as diverse as Robert Benchley, Frances Hodgson Burnett, Marc Connelly, Robert Frost, Ellen Glasgow, Sidney Howard, Walter Lippmann, Kathleen Norris, Eugene O'Neill, Edwin Arlington Robinson, and Elinor Wylie. The strength of the early membership lists was that they did not reflect any special literary set or way of writing and, in fact, none of them has ever since.

The American Center of the P.E.N. came into formal existence on Wednesday, the 19th of April, 1922. "By John Farrar's beneficent strategy" a dinner was held in the Coffee House Club, of which he was a member, and about forty people gathered in the pleasant upstairs room on West 45th Street to eat broiled shad and lamb chops and to inaugurate the Club's existence.

The President of the American Center was Booth Tarkington, who had amiably agreed to serve but who clearly had no intention of leaving his native Indiana. He sent the gathering a message of good will and it was read at the April dinner by Alexander Black, who was chairman of the Executive Committee and therefore the presiding officer for the evening.

Black noted that the membership had shown "a marked cordiality, I might say a disquieting cordiality," to the idea of not having any speeches. There was, however, one thing he wanted to say. He wanted to point out that the P.E.N. was trying to do something new and that it was worth trying. "In a quarrelsome world the plan has more than a plausibility. You may feel, as I do, that it has a kind of poetry."

Black also read a letter from Galsworthy which sent warmest greetings to the American Center and set down the limited and honorable hope upon which the P.E.N. was founded. "We writers are in some sort trustees for human nature; if we are narrow and prejudiced we harm the human race. And the better we know each other . . . the greater the chance of human happiness in a world not, as yet, too happy."

It was one of Galsworthy's basic ideas that there should be an International Congress each year to which all the Centers would send delegates. The first of these Congresses was held in 1923 in London, and Galsworthy worked untiringly to make it a success. By this time there was an impressive number of Centers, and representatives came from Belgium, Czechoslovakia, Denmark, France, Italy, Norway, Rumania, Spain, Sweden, and the United States.

Later in the year, a cable from London descended upon Alexander Black, inquiring "whether the American Center would commit itself to the holding of the next international convention of P.E.N. Clubs." After a moment of dismay the Americans rallied strongly, and by January of 1924 preparations were in full swing.

It had been decided to hold the New York Congress in May, and one of the first things to be done at the January meeting was to elect a new President for the Center—one who would be nearer at hand than Indiana. Mary Austin "nominated Mr. Carl Van Doren for President for the term of one year, to succeed Mr. Tarkington. Mr. Floyd Dell seconded. Unanimous vote for Mr. Van Doren." A flock of committees was also set up at this January meeting, and anyone who was willing to work was enthusiastically welcomed.

By March, the Executive Committee was struggling with the problem of how to finance what was currently being called a "May festival." Publishers were rounded up for financial contributions, and each of the Center's members (nearly 150 by now) was asked to donate five dollars.

The program of the New York Congress consisted of three days of festivities and discussions, and the highlight was a gala banquet held at the Hotel Pennsylvania on the 13th of May. The American hosts, who were not by nature linguists, did their best in a very international atmosphere. "Eighteen languages, literately uttered, struggled for supremacy with the hotel's knife-and-dish-dropping force." The menu had been chosen with care. There was Consommé Madrilène Mexicane to honor Octavio

Barreda of Mexico, Olives Espagnol for Amerijo Castro of Spain,
Sauce Hollandaise for Dr. Barnouw of the Netherlands, and so
on, ending with Danish pastry for Olga Ott of Denmark.

The most impressive speeches were those given by Jules
Romains of the French P.E.N. and by Chekhov's widow, who
was representing Russia. There was also a letter from Galsworthy,
which was read by Mrs. Dawson Scott. Galsworthy did not doubt
the warmth of American hospitality, which he had experienced
so often "with a wonder amounting almost to consternation."
What he wanted to emphasize in his letter was the reason behind
P.E.N. hospitality. "I beg you earnestly to believe that our meetings are not just festivity, but gestures of friendliness which have
a deep and wide-reaching significance. . . . Friends, the P.E.N.
Club was a great dream. . . . I believe I speak from your hearts,
as well as from my own, when I say: 'With this dream we will go
forward till we have made of it a great reality.' Good fortune to
you all and may you serve this dream."

Very few dreams die suddenly. Most of them just fade away.
It was the good fortune of the P.E.N. that in nearly every Center
there were writers who agreed with Galsworthy that the dream
was worth the boredom of committee meetings, the drudgery of
sending out notices, and the frustration of attending to details
of organization which were never permanently solved.

Each Center was free to organize itself in its own way, just so
long as it did not abridge the general set of principles that gov-
erned them all, and from the beginning it was clear what the
pattern of the American Center was going to be. The election of
officers would take place every year, in obedience to a principle
that had been followed from the earliest days of colonial New
England and was now so deep in the American grain that it was
almost instinctive.

Mrs. Dawson Scott grew increasingly disturbed by the American system, and in 1928 she was moved to protest. "The American P.E.N. changes its president annually, which may or may
not be a good idea; but it also appears to be going to change its
secretary, which seems to me a disastrous idea. How are we
going to have any continuity?" She suggested that if the Secretary of the American Center was "an important person" with

many demands on his time, money might be found for a part-time secretary to do some of his work for him so that he would be willing to remain in office. "It is important for the welfare of the P.E.N. that there should be some arrangement made for continuity."

The American P.E.N. sent back a soothing reply. "We have voted, anyhow, to appropriate enough money each year to pay the secretarial and accounting expenses, and this should make for stability." Nevertheless, the Center was chronically short of money, since the dues were only five dollars a year and there was no other source of income, and it continued to lurch on its hazardous way without the safeguards that Mrs. Dawson Scott would have liked.

In this it was in complete contrast to the branch of the P.E.N. in San Francisco. A California chapter had been discussed as early as 1922, and it seemed to be the perfect solution that Gertrude Atherton, a prominent novelist of the day and a great lady in her own right, was more than willing to run it. She headed the San Francisco branch when it was formed in April of 1924 and continued in office until her death nearly a quarter of a century later. When she died the San Francisco branch died with her, for it had never had any real existence of its own. Mrs. Dawson Scott had hoped for continuity by keeping the same officers. But, in the case of San Francisco, the result was a failure of energy—that mysterious commodity without which no organization can remain in existence but for which there is no formula.

During the 1920's, one of the sources of energy in the American Center was Henry Seidel Canby. He had been a "tower of strength" during the New York Congress, and when he succeeded Carl Van Doren as President of the Center he saw in the office an almost unique opportunity to foster the internationalism of which he himself dreamed.

Especially dear to his heart was the subject of translation—that indispensable bridge which links all countries, all writers and all cultures. This was, of course, a subject which was of great importance to the European Centers, and when the P.E.N. delegates gathered at the Third International Congress, which was

held in Paris in 1925, it was decided "to give the question of
translations particular attention."

It was suggested specifically that every Center "might compile
lists of books which ought to be translated into other languages
and make a register of competent translators," and this idea
seemed so hopeful that a serious effort was made to persuade
the Carnegie Endowment for International Peace to support it.
Finally, a member of the American Center came up with an
alternative suggestion, and Canby presented it formally when he
served as delegate to the P.E.N. Congress in Brussels in June of
1927.

The idea was to set up, preferably in Paris, "an international
clearing house of literary information to simplify, clarify, speed
and make more efficient to everyone concerned—author, publisher and public—the flow of literary expression across language
frontiers." The Brussels Congress gave the idea its enthusiastic
approval and set up a sub-committee consisting of Canby, Galsworthy, Mrs. Dawson Scott, and the International Secretary of
P.E.N. whose name was Hermon Ould. Canby was so sure of
success that he talked with the directors of the League of International Cooperation in Geneva and was promised the use of
part of the Palais Royal in Paris to serve as headquarters for the
proposed translation bureau.

The scheme was based in part on the financial support of the
publishers, who would pay an annual fee for the use of the facil-
ities of the clearing house. By August, six London publishers
had pledged their support, and the following month Hermon
Ould rounded up fourteen publishers in Germany. In October,
Canby appealed to American publishers, and in general the
response was both prompt and favorable. John Macrae of Dutton's, who had a Scotch dislike of spending money unnecessarily,
ended his long letter on the problems faced by a small publishing
house by suddenly announcing that he would be delighted to
join and that the fee of fifty dollars was very reasonable. William
Morrow, who also headed a small house, agreed. "This is an
altruistic scheme of the type that I like to support."

By the spring of 1928, the American Center had managed to
collect in various ways the sum of $6,500. This was an impres-

sive amount but a long way from the three thousand pounds that Galsworthy felt would be necessary "to support the office and carry on the work with vigour and efficiency." Talks and interviews continued, but it soon became clear that the P.E.N. was too young and too loosely organized to be able to turn so ambitious a dream into reality. As Canby put it, the idea "finally came to nothing, partly because it was impossible to raise the necessary money and partly because it became clear that the P.E.N. Clubs as a whole had not a sufficient central organization to guarantee the proper support and control."

He remained hopeful, however. He agreed in 1933 to be a delegate to the P.E.N. Congress in Yugoslavia, and he asked the American Center to think over possible proposals in connection with translation which he might discuss with a sub-committee of the League of Nations. Perhaps the P.E.N. could "cooperate with the League committee in handling the vexed question of translations from one language to another."

The Yugoslav Congress of 1933 was held at Dubrovnik, that ancient city on the sea, circled by walls and backed by mountains. It was a beautiful and peaceful place, but Canby knew before he arrived that questions like translation would probably find no place in it. In fact, the international atmosphere had become so threatening and the basic principles of P.E.N. were so clearly at stake that the membership of the American Center held a lunch meeting on the third of May to discuss what kind of resolution ought to be presented at this Congress. One of the suggested resolutions even went to the extreme of stating that Canby should be "empowered to withdraw the American Center if the international principles of the organization are in his judgment not upheld." The final decision, however, was to send Canby to Dubrovnik with a long and carefully worded resolution which reaffirmed the basic international principles of the P.E.N.

These principles had always existed in theory, but it was over the years, at the annual P.E.N. Congresses, that they had been worked out in practice. An impressive early example of this was the Berlin Congress of 1926, the "first international congress of any kind to be held in Berlin since the Armistice." Romain Rolland and André Gide both attended it, and it was an expression of the brotherhood to which Thomas Mann had already testified. Mann was the first German writer to be a guest of honor of the English P.E.N., and he never forgot "the generous kindness" that welcomed him, the alien and the former enemy, into the company of his fellow writers.

After the Berlin Congress of 1926, Galsworthy wrote out a formal statement which he thought might "serve as a touchstone of P.E.N. action" in any future time of trouble:

1. Literature, national though it be in origin, knows no frontiers, and should remain common currency between nations in spite of political or international upheavals.
2. In all circumstances, and particularly in time of war, works of art, the patrimony of humanity at large, should be left untouched by national or political passion.
3. Members of the P.E.N. will at all times use what influence they have in favour of good understanding and mutual respect between nations.

When the next P.E.N. Congress met in 1927 at Brussels, this resolution was presented with the combined backing of the Belgian, English, French and German delegations and passed without difficulty.

The American delegate to this Brussels Congress of 1927 was Henry Seidel Canby, and since he was an experienced internationalist he had very little difficulty with the language problem. The following year, the Congress was held at Oslo, and this time the delegate was Henry Goddard Leach. Leach was not skilled in either French or German, which, along with English, were the official languages of the Congress, but he enjoyed himself thoroughly. In 1931 he wrote the current delegates from the American Center to assure them they would have a good time, and he added: "I predict that you will start some life friendships at this Congress. Only today I answered a letter from the African delegate to the P.E.N. conference in Oslo."

Good will was everything, surmounting all the language difficulties and serving as the best of translators. Alexander Black remembered how he had felt, back in the days of the New York Congress of 1924, when he found himself stranded "in a vast floor space with Jules Romains. . . . Romains had no English and my French was (and is) deplorable. . . . The odd thing is (I'd hate to have to prove it) that Romains and I *talked*."

Will Irwin went as delegate to the Warsaw Congress of 1930, and he came back delighted. These Congresses were becoming very elaborate, now that P.E.N. was being taken with increasing seriousness by the heads of state, but the Polish Center had managed to combine the formal ceremonies with some very easy-going moments. Irwin especially enjoyed an "elaborate luncheon with many subtle drinks" which was followed by lying around under the trees and eating cherries and strawberries.

The day that pleased Irwin the most started with a boat trip on the great river of Poland, the Vistula. The P.E.N. delegates sat under arches of green boughs, decorated with flowers and the flags of the various nations, and they slipped peacefully past ancient castles and great forests until they were suddenly hit by a cloudburst. The soaked delegates were entertained by a Polish countess who had originally planned to give them tea but who, under the circumstances, thoughtfully included "much cognac and not a little vodka." They danced for an hour to warm themselves and then went on their hilarious way, wrapped in blankets and singing in twenty languages. They were due at a banquet given by the Governor of the province, but only a few were able to dress the part. The ladies of the Austrian delegation managed to appear in evening dress, and one of the Danes had a dinner coat. "They were roundly applauded. Behind them—and this brought the house to its feet—came two of the Englishmen in Turkish-towel bathrobes and another . . . in a pair of robin's-egg-blue pyjamas kindly loaned by the management."

No Russian delegates were present, although it was just the sort of convivial occasion that would have delighted them. The P.E.N. had grown weary, for the moment at least, of trying to persuade the Russians to form a Center. As the International Secretary pointed out, they had been issued an invitation "five separate and distinct times" and nothing had happened.

If anyone could have persuaded the Russians to join it would have been the International Secretary, the wise and patient Hermon Ould. Ould had been a conscientious objector during the

War, and this had wrecked his career as a playwright. He was
present at the inaugural dinner of the P.E.N. in London in 1921,
but he did not have enough money to go to many of the following ones. He believed ardently, however, in what the organization was trying to do and, as he said, he "slipped into the position of English Secretary. . . . I found myself doing the job because there was nobody else to do it." The same thing happened
with the post of International General Secretary, to which he
was formally elected at the Berlin Congress of 1926. After that
Ould remained in the post of International Secretary, just as
Galsworthy remained in the post of International President.
The delegates to the Congresses might not agree on other matters,
but they agreed on the value of these two remarkable men, who
by their single-hearted devotion were building the P.E.N., year
by year, to an increasing eminence.

The 1931 Congress was held in Amsterdam, and by this time
the P.E.N. really had the right to call itself a worldwide organization. There were delegates not only from most of the countries of Europe but also from Australia, Canada, China, and South
America. Hopeful overtures to India and Japan had not yet come
to anything, but when the Amsterdam Congress issued its
"Appeal to all Governments" it could claim a right to be heard.
"We, undersigned members or honorary members of the non-
political World Association of Writers called the P.E.N., representing some four thousand writers in thirty-five countries, respectfully draw the attention of all governments to . . . the ill-
treatment . . . of people imprisoned on political or religious
grounds."

This same Congress of 1931 also passed a set of bylaws, and
Article II was a reiteration of the three points that Galsworthy
had drafted "as a touchstone of P.E.N. action" and which had
been approved at Brussels. For the rest, the delegates had the
pleasure of being entertained in the beautiful old city of Amsterdam, in the company of fellow delegates like Halldor Laxness,
Karel Capek and Sholem Asch.

The following year the Congress was scheduled to meet in
Budapest. By this time the political situation had become so
troubled that Galsworthy began to wonder if the meeting ought

to be postponed. However, it had become "almost an axiom of the P.E.N. never to postpone anything," and the Budapest Congress of 1932 was held as planned.

It was a glittering affair. Admiral Horthy, as head of state, gave a reception for the P.E.N. that was Old Europe at its most magnificent. This reception was held in the Royal Palace, with its almost nine hundred rooms, and Galsworthy, who never liked ceremony, had to make his patient way, in an atmosphere stiff with protocol, under vast chandeliers and through a sea of footmen. Joseph Anthony, who happened to be in Budapest at the time, went to the state dinner for the P.E.N. and to the official receptions, and he noted that "the transformation from the first simple meetings in London was startling."

In January of the following year, 1933, John Galsworthy died, leaving the money from his Nobel Prize in a trust fund for the P.E.N. It was his final gift to the organization he had loved and sustained, and he had good reason to feel that it had justified his time and his devotion.

His successor in the office of International President was H. G. Wells, a writer of a very different temperament. Wells was tough and lively and delighted in a fight, being willing to tackle any parliamentary problem in his bad French and with the aid of his British common sense. It was fortunate that he did not frighten easily, for his first Congress as President was the one held at Dubrovnik in 1933.

During the same month in which Galsworthy died, Adolf Hitler became Chancellor of Germany, and a short time later an obedient Reichstag voted to give him the powers of a dictator. Hitler knew that there was no greater threat to his authority than the writers of Germany, those who upheld the strength of the spirit while he upheld the power of the sword. Many of them were self-exiled by now and beyond his reach, but, if he could not destroy them, he could at least destroy what they had written.

On the tenth of May, 1933, six cities of Germany were the simultaneous scene of six great ceremonial bonfires—the Burning of the Books. It was one of the most sinister moments of that tormented decade, since it served notice to all free minds that

their existence was the enemy of the new German state. John
Milton, in his attack on censorship in *Areopagitica,* had described a good book as "the precious life blood of a master
spirit . . . treasured up on purpose to a life beyond life." It was
Hitler's intention to turn this life into death.

Two weeks later, the P.E.N. Congress was held at Dubrovnik,
and as soon as the delegates from the German Center arrived it
was clear that they had been given their instructions. The
leader of the delegation was the author of a campaign life of
Hitler, and the rest of the delegation was equally satisfactory
from the Nazi point of view.

There was only one American delegate at Dubrovnik. But
this one was Henry Seidel Canby, and he brought with him the
very carefully worded resolution that had been drafted by the
Executive Committee of the American Center, "especially Will
Irwin, Robert Nathan and Alfred Dashiell." It opened with
a general statement of principle: "Whereas there are again
abroad in the world aspects of chauvinism which debase the
spirit of man, causing him to persecute his fellow men, robbing
him of generosity, of nobility, and understanding; and whereas
it is the duty of the artist to guard the spirit in its freedom, so
that mankind shall not be prey to ignorance, to malice and to
fear, we the members of the American Center of the P.E.N. call
upon all other centers to affirm once more those principles
upon which the structure of this society was raised."

The resolution continued with a repetition of the three points
approved at Brussels in 1927 and incorporated in the bylaws in
1931. It closed with what was in effect an open attack upon the
German Center, which had been removing from its membership
all Jews, all liberals, all writers of any kind who were not willing
to support the new German state. "We likewise call upon the
International Congress to take definite steps to prevent the individual centers of the P.E.N., founded for the purpose of foster-
ing goodwill and understanding between the races and nations,
from being used as weapons of propaganda in the defence of
persecution inflicted in the name of chauvinism, racial prejudice
and political ill-will."

This was the resolution that H. G. Wells chose from among many to present to the Congress at the opening meeting. It passed unanimously, the German delegates voting with the rest. The words were only words, and the Germans evidently dismissed them as vague rhetoric. The proper thing, from their point of view, would have been to continue with the usual Congress agenda, with literary papers to be read and discussed. Instead, these papers "were unread." The delegates knew that they faced a direct challenge, one that could not be dismissed with a few remarks on international brotherhood.

The following morning, the battle had a clear focus. Ernst Toller had been invited to be one of the speakers at the Congress and his name was on the agenda. A very fine playwright, Toller was one of the growing number of writers who were exiles from Germany. He was a Jew, a radical, a former Communist; the German delegation was determined that he should not be permitted to speak.

This attempt to silence Toller was one of the first signs of the deadly creeping movement of the Nazis outside the borders of their own country, and as soon as the question came up the Congress erupted. Some of the delegations feared the Germans too much to oppose them, and a member from one of the oldest and bravest governments in Europe shrieked: "The future is Germany's. You must yield." Wells, unperturbed by the tumult, put the question to the vote, and it was the will of the majority that Toller be permitted to speak.

There was a frenzy of both hissing and cheering in the little opera house where the meeting was being held, and the German delegation rose and walked out of the building. Toller gave his speech, but Canby did not hear it. He could not put his mind on anything except what he had just seen—"visible fear rising like a cold fire."

Toller's speech, in fact, was on the subject of fear, which he had lived with for a long time. He reminded his fellow writers that the German delegation had voted the previous day for a resolution which affirmed that it was the duty of the artist to keep the spirit free so that humanity "does not become the

prey of ignorance, of evil and of fear." He gave the list, name by
name, of the fifty-eight writers whose books had been burned on
the tenth of May, and he suggested that if the German Center was
in earnest it would come to the aid of the writers whom Hitler
was trying to destroy. At the end of his speech, Toller said:
"I question whether we will again find an opportunity to con-
vene and talk together in the Europe of today because he who
rebels is doomed. Who cares? Let us conquer the fear which
crushes and humbles us."

It was a much more magnificent Congress than the one held
the previous year. In Budapest, there had been the glitter and
panoply of state approval, with all the elegance and respectabil-
ity that Admiral Horthy could supply. In Dubrovnik, there
were individual writers alone with their consciences, and the
great majority refused to deny the principle upon which the
P.E.N. had been founded. They would not let themselves be
corrupted by fear. Years later, a French writer who had been at
Dubrovnik spoke of this Congress as an event in the intellectual
history of Europe. It was also an event in the history of P.E.N.
It proved that its members had agreed to a basic principle which
they would not betray, no matter how frightening the present
or how unclear the future. They would follow Toller's way and
not Hitler's.

The International Executive Committee was scheduled to
meet in November, and the Canby resolution ended by empower-
ing the Committee to "take action if . . . any P.E.N. center has
failed to conform with these principles." Canby himself was convinced that "the Germans will return to the fold in November,"
and it was true that the President of the German Center put up
an energetic defense at the London meeting of the Committee.
Nevertheless, he was obliged to admit that the Center had removed all members "who supported Communist or similar
views" and that by the latter was meant "several shades of
liberal opinion." A resolution was offered to the Committee,
proposed by Mrs. Dawson Scott and seconded by Will Irwin,
that the German Center had violated a basic principle of P.E.N.
by "interference in the political views of its members." Only
the President of the German Center voted against it, and when

he found he was defeated, he left the meeting to circulate a report that the P.E.N. had turned Communist.

Many people were willing to believe that any organization which was anti-Nazi was therefore pro-Communist, and it was true that there had been many attempts to bring the writers of Russia into the P.E.N. The year after the Congress at Dubrovnik, H. G. Wells, as International President, sent a message to the Soviet Writers Congress that the P.E.N. "would like to see a Russian P.E.N. Club established." Nevertheless, he was careful to repeat the basic principle which every Center must accept: it must be "freely open to competent writers of whatever shade of political or social opinion they may be," and it must be "a self-governing body entirely independent of any governmental or official control." This stipulation was an impossible one for Stalin's Russia just as it had been for Hitler's Germany. In fact, P.E.N. was finding itself with less and less space in a world that was hardening into an increasing respect for the absolute power of the totalitarian state.

Back in 1931, an anxious member of the American Center wrote to Hermon Ould: "At a time when the world is so upset it seems to me that the P.E.N. should become a force, if it is ever to be. . . . Otherwise it would seem that we are doomed to be a social club." The P.E.N. was becoming a force almost in spite of itself, simply by refusing to abandon its allegiance to the freedom of the human spirit.

It did not, of course, cease to be a "social club." This was the fabric upon which its existence rested, since otherwise the members would have had no way of meeting one another. Each Center had its own way of providing fellowship, and in the case of the American Center the usual method was through a series of dinner meetings.

When the American Center held its first meeting in 1922, there had been no speeches, but this was a policy that varied according to the occasion. When Galsworthy attended a dinner meeting in 1926, the membership naturally wanted to hear him talk, and since he was the International President this was a situation to which he had to resign himself. In this same year, however, John Masefield was promised that a dinner in his honor at

the Brevoort would have "friends present but no speeches." Two
months later, there was a dinner to honor three writers from
England, and it was announced that there would be "no formal
speeches, although there may be one or two brief informal talks."
The three English writers were Ford Madox Ford, Osbert Sitwell
and Hugh Walpole. In the audience there was even more variety,
since it included the author of that hardy juvenile perennial,
Beautiful Joe.

During this period of the 1920's, it was the custom to honor
foreign writers only. As the Executive Committee of the American
Center put it in 1927: "The giving of dinners to American authors
is a dangerous thing." Apparently the Committee did not wish
to put itself in the position of honoring one local author rather
than another; it did decide to give a dinner for Booth Tarkington
"because he lives in Indianapolis," but there is no record that he
came. In April of 1929, however, there was a dinner at the
Commodore which was also a reception for new members, and
the guests of honor included John Dewey, Sinclair Lewis, Don
Marquis, Lewis Mumford, Dorothy Thompson, and Thornton
Wilder.

Lewis had been invited to join the previous January, and he
wrote that he would be happy to accept membership. "I know
the P.E.N. Club very well in England, France and Germany. But
please do not have me as guest of honor at any time." He agreed
to attend the dinner in April, for which two English speakers had
been planned, and sat at Table One. The following year he received the Nobel Prize—the first American writer to do so—and Will
Irwin, as President of the American Center, called Lewis's publisher to sound him out on the possibility of a speech. Alfred
Harcourt was obliged to report that the last words he had heard
from his distinguished author were, "For God's sake, Alfred,
don't let anyone give me a dinner!"

The basic rule of any successful P.E.N. President is never to
take "no" for an answer, and Will Irwin was very persuasive. In
the end Sinclair Lewis not only consented to a P.E.N. dinner in
his honor but he delivered a vigorous speech. By a coincidence,
the only other non-European to be given a Nobel Prize in Literature—Rabindranath Tagore of India—was also in New York

giving a speech at a banquet. Both men attacked the same thing, a materialistic contempt for the things of the spirit, and Lewis's speech was barbed. "I shall list for you the important things in America. First there is business; the Great God Business. The manufacturer of a carburetor is manifestly more important than any manufacturer of poetry." He implored writers to take themselves seriously, if no one else would, and, to make it clear that by seriousness he did not mean solemnity, Lewis gave P. G. Wodehouse as an example of a writer who did. His speech maddened the newspapers as it was intended to do, and an editorial scolded him for his message while simultaneously failing to understand what it was.

The "Great God Business" was in trouble in America, and in 1932 the American P.E.N. could congratulate itself on the fact that its members were still able to pay their dues. "Our membership has as yet not suffered as a result of the Depression and we still have more than 200 members." In fact, the shortage of money had not even affected the price that was being asked for the dinners, and one member was moved to protest. "Don't you think $3.50 a little high to charge for a dinner . . .? Or hasn't the Brevoort heard about the hard times?" By 1935, the price of the dinner had dropped to $1.75, and the charge was two dollars the following year when the P.E.N. dinners moved to the Algonquin.

These dinners, as they had been from the first, were handled rather formally. Place cards were supplied, dinner jackets were expected, and the Algonquin was able to supply such items as green turtle soup with sherry as part of the two-dollar dinner. The guest of honor, for his part, often felt his social responsibilities keenly. Hilaire Belloc, for instance, wrote an apologetic letter in 1935 to explain why he would not be wearing his "evening coat." It had been sent to be mended and would not be back in time.

The committee in charge of the dinners encountered the usual woes that are endemic to this particular occupation. The seating arrangements, for instance, were almost certain to have something wrong with them. "I am a new member. . . . Don't put me with anyone who is seven years older than God." The guest

of honor, even after he had been cornered, was sometimes hard
to keep track of. As one lecture agent said soothingly, "Artistic
gentlemen seldom handle their mail promptly." But he was sure
that the artistic gentleman in question intended to come to the
P.E.N. dinner. "Take the time to write him another letter,
giving him the place, the date and the hour. He probably has
lost his instructions by now."

Sometimes it was difficult to persuade the members themselves to come to the dinner, and then the only thing to do was
to telephone around. "A bad start came through to a good finish.
We had 52 at dinner finally." On the other hand, the night that
Eleanor Roosevelt was the speaker, 125 people came and were
wholly content. A foreign member said that it was an evening
he would never forget, and Frank Case of the Algonquin rose to
the occasion with a perfect dinner, perfectly served. By this
time, the Algonquin had been obliged to increase the price of
the dinners slightly but was including flowers. As for the earlier
P.E.N. policy of not using American writers on the program, it
had wholly ceased. In fact, as the Program Chairman said in
February of 1938, "We are especially anxious to bring more of
our own members into the program rather than depending
entirely on visiting foreign writers."

The Program Chairman was Bessie Beatty, a journalist and
editor who had been a member since 1924. She gave the dinners
her careful attention, and they were both lively and imaginative.
As Henry Goddard Leach put it in 1937: "P.E.N. is moving along
in fine shape with a series of spirited meetings." The following
year, Bessie Beatty was elected Secretary, the first woman to
hold that office, and she accepted the post, as she said, "with
many misgivings and a terrific sense of responsibility."

She had good reason. For, by this time, the American Center
was heavily involved in a plan to be host to an international
meeting of writers in New York in 1939, and it was Bessie Beatty
who was expected to run it.

There was to be a World's Fair in New York in 1939, and the
directors of the Fair felt it would be desirable to publicize the
event among foreign writers. They were willing to invest ten
thousand dollars in this project, which would pay for the housing

and entertainment of delegates if the American Center would
hold a P.E.N. Congress in New York to coincide with the Fair's
opening.

When Henry Seidel Canby went as a delegate to the Paris
Congress of 1937, he brought with him a cordial invitation from
the head of the World's Fair: "I take great pleasure in inviting
the members of this Congress to be our guests." It turned out
that the Congress for 1939 had already been promised to Stockholm, but the Swedish Center obligingly agreed to shift its date
to the autumn of 1939 so that a kind of unofficial World's Fair
Congress of writers could be held in New York in the spring.

There were difficulties from the beginning. The invitation
that Canby brought with him had been so loosely worded that
it sounded as though the delegates would have their transportation paid. It was natural to think so, for the previous P.E.N.
Congress, that of 1936, had been held in Buenos Aires. Since
it had been supported by the government, both the official
delegates and their wives had had their transportation paid, and
surely the rich North Americans could be planning to do no less.

The World's Fair would not pay transportation. The American
Center could not and, in fact, was not even able to persuade
the steamship lines to give special rates. But the French Center
was convinced that Canby had personally promised free transportation, and it took a long time to mollify its infuriated Secretary.
Bessie Beatty wrote Hermon Ould, only a month before the Congress was due to open, to say that there had been a great deal of
misunderstanding of Canby's invitation, which was no less than
the truth. By this time she was deep in a variety of complications; she told Ould that she had covered the Russian Revolution
in 1919 but that this was much more exhausting.

The root of her difficulties was that she had the responsibility
for running the Congress without the authority. Any decision
she made had to have the approval of the Executive Committee,
which was difficult to get together and not very energetic.

A cooperative President would have been a great help, but
here again the American Center was in trouble. Since 1931 there
had been only two Presidents, Robert Frost and Dorothy Thompson, and neither was wholly satisfactory. Frost had been per-

suaded to serve by his good friend, Frederic Melcher, but only
as an honorary President, and Frost's impression of his duties
was so vague that even when he did turn up at a dinner meeting
he had no thought of presiding. Dorothy Thompson succeeded
him in 1936, and since she had a very different temperament,
she presided over the dinner meetings with energy and grace. But
she was an enormously busy woman, at the height of her international reputation, and Bessie Beatty found it was very difficult
to get her attention.

All the letters of invitation to the World's Fair Congress and
all the letters asking for financial contributions had to go out
over Dorothy Thompson's signature, and there were naturally
many other areas where the President of the Center could not
properly be bypassed. In February of 1939, only five months
before the Congress was due to open, Miss Beatty was still
battling for her attention. "Every possible representation has
been made to her three secretaries, but they all say that when
they tell her something must be done about P.E.N., Dorothy
replies that she wanted to resign and we wouldn't let her."
Four days later, Miss Beatty tried a direct approach: "I hate to
pester you, but I am forced to repeat that the first free time in
your crowded program is due me." She herself was working on
a volunteer basis but she had the services of a paid assistant, and
the following month he, in his turn, had a try at one of Miss
Thompson's secretaries. "If you can manage even a fifteen-
minute appointment for Miss Beatty, I believe it would be most
helpful. You can have only a remote idea of the details and endless questions from all countries that pour in on us here."

Other complications included a snarl of red tape with the
World's Fair, struggles with the steamship lines and confusion
with the delegates. "Many of our expected guests have not informed us what boats they will arrive on; in consequence, we
must watch the shipping news, then rush to meet them at the
pier." The Customs Service refused to issue a general pass, so
this was one more small complication in a situation already
bristling with them.

At the end of April, with the tickets waiting to be printed
giving the location of the official ceremonies, it began to look

as though there would be no location at all. The Hall of Music at the Fair was under the control of General Motors, which suddenly decided not to permit the P.E.N. to use it. An urgent appeal went out to the head of the Fair: "Need your help in desperate dilemma." Strings were pulled frantically, and General Motors consented to reverse its decision. The tickets were printed, and one more crisis was surmounted.

As was usual in the American Center whenever there was a real need, a great many members worked hard to make the occasion a success. There was a proliferation of committees, and most of them were well run. Everything which had been planned for the pleasure of the delegates took place, although Miss Beatty's assistant, faced with what he called a "wholesale changing of minds," remarked that he had not known so much confusion since the stock-market crash of 1929.

None of this anxious scurrying around behind scenes showed itself in the end, and the week's program went off smoothly in an atmosphere of real fellowship. The opening session in the Hall of Music took place on Monday morning, the eighth of May. Walt Whitman was present in spirit, for the session closed with a reading of his salute to the people of the world in *Leaves of Grass,* his "Salut au Monde." "Health to you! Good will to you all. . . . I have look'd for equals and lovers, and found them ready for me in all lands."

There were five of these sessions, morning and afternoon, climaxed by the sixth which was a formal banquet on Wednesday evening at the Plaza Hotel. Thursday, there was a visit to Washington, where the delegates met President Roosevelt in his office and were given lunch by Mrs. Roosevelt, a fellow member of P.E.N. The entertainments in New York included a showing of Robert Sherwood's current play, *Abe Lincoln in Illinois,* and the delegates particularly enjoyed a final weekend when they were guests in various country houses in Connecticut. Bessie Beatty had a right to feel that her efforts had been worthwhile, for there was the kind of fellowship that Galsworthy had wanted every Congress to have—even a slightly irregular and unofficial Congress such as this one.

There was also something more. For this Congress took place in the last days before the outbreak of World War II, and the shadow that had shown itself at Dubrovnik was beginning to darken all Europe. As Hermon Ould said in this May of 1939, the P.E.N. stood as a spokesman for freedom. "We are 5000 strong; we have the respect of the greater part of the world; we have achieved the great honour of being mentioned and condemned as a band of Communists and Jews by Herr Goebbels, and we exist in every country where freedom of expression is still allowed."

This was the basic reason for the Congress in New York—the necessity of reaffirming the right to speak and to differ in a world where it seemed to be vanishing. One of the many writers who were invited to come and who could not was Sean O'Casey. As he said, his finances were in even worse condition than those of the P.E.N. But he sent a long letter, and it was one which showed very clearly that he understood what the Congress was about.

> Never fear, I have always and always will fight, in my own way (a pretty vigorous way) for the right of all to speak, to publish, to assemble, and to worship—ay, and the right, too, to do none of these things, if some be so minded; ay, and the right, too, to refuse to worship things that some believe to be stupid, reactionary, or brutal. But fair-minded men and women are threatened now, not exactly with suppression, but actually with annihilation. So now it is not so much a fight for freedom of speech as it is a fight for our lives. So, fighting for our lives, we have to use that force which is used against us—we have to force the oppressor to allow us to face him, and say out what we have to say. That is why, I think, that there should be a swift union of all forces in all the democracies, and, indeed, in all countries that desire that Peace from which alone, at long last, truth will come from the clashing thought of all decent and intelligent human minds. God be with your Conference.

Many of the writers who gathered in New York this week in May were already exiles—men like Toller and Mann of Germany and Borgese of Italy. Some, if they went home again, could find only concentration camps or death. The year before, the

P.E.N. Congress had been held in Prague; Czechoslovakia had
seemed very safe, and Eduard Benes had given the delegates
special honor. Now Benes was in exile, Prague was occupied
and betrayed, and by the end of the year the Minister of Education, who had been so graceful a host to the Congress, was dead
of torture. Jules Romains was International President of P.E.N.,
and he spoke of Prague when he gave his opening address at the
New York Congress. "We are no longer able to act as if tyranny
did not exist. Therefore, we must act that it shall not exist."

The writers who had gathered in New York refused to doubt
their power, because it was the power of the human spirit. As
one of the representatives from South America—Carlos Davila of
Chile—pointed out, it was the writers who had helped destroy
the power of Spain in that continent. "A citizen of Colombia
. . . was jailed for translating the Declaration of Independence,"
but in the end that citizen became President of his country.

Even under the current and much more terrible tyranny in
Europe, the sword could not silence the word. As Ernst Toller
said in his speech that same day: "In spite of his hangmen, Mr.
Hitler cannot prevent a dangerous spectre going about in Germany: the voice of the outlawed writer." One of these outlaws
was Thomas Mann, and Mann ended his own speech almost
with a sense of gratitude that the lines were now clearly drawn.
"This is a time of great simplification, a time when we humbly
acknowledge the difference between good and evil. . . . And
all that the times call on us to bear of anguish is outweighed by
the youthful joy of the spirit, at finding itself once more in its
chosen role: the role of David against Goliath, of Saint George
against the old Dragon of violence and lies."

Time magazine, which had evidently never heard of the
Dubrovnik Congress, announced that after "17 years of its
decorous, soft-spoken existence" the P.E.N. had at last charged
into action. What it really meant was that this was the first
time P.E.N. had had a New York audience. All the speeches
were broadcast over the radio, and General Motors was apparently
not altogether pleased to find itself playing host to so single-
minded a group. When it finally gave reluctant permission to
have the Hall of Music used by P.E.N., the letter came from the

Public Relations Department, and one sentence in it seems to
indicate what had been the original difficulty in getting the use
of the auditorium. "In view of the controversial nature of the
subject under discussion, I am counting on you to avoid any
mention of General Motors over the air." To be controversial
was to be anti-business, and this was a business fair.

A columnist for one of the New York papers was amused to
note what he felt was a lack of contemporary reality in the
speeches. He said that the writers with their cries of warning
were still living in the Middle Ages and that the more truthful
view belonged to General Motors, with its shiny display that
was called Futurama. In support of this theory, he pointed out
that there were always long lines in front of the General Motors
exhibit, while in the Hall of Music that held the P.E.N. sessions
half the seats were empty.

The truth has never been very popular, and it was not popular
now. Nevertheless, the writers had their say, speaking the truth
as they saw it—the truth, as O'Casey said, of "decent and intelligent human minds."

Back in 1922, when the American Center was founded, a newspaper report of the event started off with a quotation: *"Le coeur
n'a pas de pays."* It was this conviction that the heart has no
country, this international fellowship in a time of great fear, that
was the best justification for the World's Fair Congress of 1939
and, in fact, for the P.E.N. itself.

Part Two

The International P.E.N. Congress of 1939 was due to open in Stockholm on the third of September, having been postponed so that New York could have its meeting in the spring. There was a "great cargo of writers leaving from England," which included E. M. Forster, Stefan Zweig and H. G. Wells. Wells was no longer International President, since the term was now a limited one, but he was as pugnacious as ever and had prepared "a provocative address."

Bessie Beatty was the official delegate from the American Center, and she was still finishing the last details that remained from the World's Fair Congress the night before she sailed for Europe on a Polish liner. She never reached Stockholm. Her ship dodged a Nazi submarine for five days in the North Sea, and she finally landed in England just in time to hear war declared.

P.E.N.'s International Secretary, Hermon Ould, had spent eighteen months during World War I in a cell in Dartmoor as a conscientious objector, and nothing had changed his conviction that war was a very great evil. But he also knew that everything he valued would cease to exist unless Hitler could be stopped. Ould no longer trusted in what he now called "the fallacy of absolutes in morals. . . . One had to choose the less harmful, according to one's lights." He was equally sure, how-

ever, that a writer would only darken his own light and be of
no real service to anyone if he permitted himself the same evil
weapons as the enemy.

The President of the English Center was Storm Jameson, the
first woman to be chosen for the office in England and only
after a certain amount of argument. She felt as Ould did, and
on the 25th of September the English Center issued a statement
to counteract a call for total warfare from some of the super-
patriots. "A writer who persuades us to hate is ensuring that
we are unfit to make peace. One of his tasks is to keep us sane."
A year later, in August of 1940 when the bombs were raining
on London, this position was reiterated. "We are not fighting
only for ourselves, but for the belief we share with every man of
any race and religion, who holds that men should respect each
other and minds should be free. . . . In as much as we are fighting for the consciences of our children, we are fighting for the
people of every nation. . . . We do not desire and we will set
our faces against revenge."

In every country, the writers had been among the first to
speak out against tyranny. In Italy, for instance, the Secretary
of the P.E.N. Center in Rome, who was a poet and the son of a
translator of poetry, "acquired an aeroplane, loaded it with leaflets revealing the true nature of the Fascist tyranny, flew over
Rome and scattered the leaflets all over the city . . . then turned
in his tracks, flew in the direction of the sea, and was never seen
again." As one country after another was overrun, the writers who
were able to escape took refuge in the nations that were still
free, but after Paris fell there was almost no shelter left. In July
of 1940, the English Center was obliged to report: "We are now
cut off from Austria, Czechoslovakia, Poland, Denmark, Norway,
Holland, Belgium and France; and communication with most
other European countries has become all but impossible."

The P.E.N. Centers of Europe did not cease to exist. Its members made their way to England, those of them who could, and
re-formed in London. Even before the war broke out, when
Austria was overrun, its P.E.N. Center re-created itself in London
with Franz Werfel as its President. In September of 1941, an
official International Congress was held in London, and the

writers of thirty-two nations were able to attend it. They were all living in England now, the only place of freedom left to them.

Three years later, in August of 1944, the English Center decided to celebrate the tercentenary of the publication of Milton's *Areopagitica*. That morning, the place where Ould had planned to hold the symposium had nearly been destroyed by a flying bomb. "When E. M. Forster and I surveyed the hall, with its broken windows, scattered masonry and blasted doors, we did ask ourselves whether we ought to carry on. That audience would have been surprised if we hadn't. . . . After all, if you're dead, you're dead, and if you're alive you've got to carry on."

In the midst of the broken glass and to the sound of carpenters putting back the windows, the P.E.N. met with other groups to pay tribute to Milton and to the idea on which he had based his great pamphlet. It was "the idea that the human mind, if it is to develop to the full measure of its potentialities, must be free to grow, free to express itself, free to blunder, to make mistakes, and try again." It was the spirit that Sean O'Casey had evoked in his letter to the New York Congress, and this basic principle behind the P.E.N. was magnificently stated by Forster in his opening address at the London symposium.

> P.E.N. is an international body. This cannot be said too often at a moment when internationalism is unfashionable. . . . We are a world association of writers, not an association of British or even of allied writers. We stand for the creative impulse which existed before nationality was invented, and which will continue to exist when that dubious invention has been scrapped. We stand for all humanity, apart from the accidents of government, language, race and colour, and we must recall our position before we start talking.

The English P.E.N. survived the war with its goals clear and its spirit without hate, and this was a very great achievement. If Galsworthy could have seen what had grown out of his relatively placid dream of an international brotherhood, he would have been very proud. He would have had less reason to be proud of the American Center.

Perhaps one explanation for the comparative failure of the American Center during the war years can be found in a very sterile decision that was made in 1939. A small amount of money was left over from the World's Fair Congress, and Bessie Beatty suggested that it might be used to set up what she called a Fellowship Committee to help the refugee writers who were already pouring into New York. "P.E.N. might take a room adjoining my office where at least once a week, Spaniards, Germans and the rest could come in for a drink, advice, etc. and meet Americans who would follow through with personal invitations and help." The suggestion was turned down, and the small sums of money went back to their donors—men like Bernard Baruch, Marshall Field and Henry Morgenthau who could hardly be said to need them.

The American Center lost a magnificent opportunity to set up a meeting place where European writers could come and where their fellow writers in America could find them. Once the war broke out, the suggestion that Bessie Beatty had made a few months earlier became even more valuable. The volume of refugees increased, but the American Center had no way to take care of them.

It was not ill will that killed the idea of the Fellowship Committee. It was rather a slackening of energy, a weakness that had been increasingly in evidence all through the 1930's in spite of the hard work of individual members. When Herman Ould wrote to congratulate Miss Beatty on the success of the World's Fair Congress, he added: "I can see very clearly that you have a hard task in New York to keep the P.E.N. going, but I hope that the interest stimulated by the congress will be a safeguard against the demise of your centre."

Part of the problem lay in the fact that this was a time of confusion for many Americans. It was not for them, as it was for men like Thomas Mann, a "time of great simplification." Ever since the beginning of Hitler's rise to power, there had been endless arguments in the United States over what ought to be done, and the members of the P.E.N. were no more in agreement than anyone else. Back in 1938, the American Center had been asked to join other organizations in support of an economic boycott of Germany, and Bessie Beatty, as Secretary, sent out three questions: "Should P.E.N. take an official stand? Would you wish to act as an individual? Do you wish both individual and official action?"

Not many members replied, but among those who did the tone was passionate and there was a large area of disagreement. Most of them felt that P.E.N. should not take action in such matters, and one member felt so strongly on this point that she wrote two letters to make her position clear. She emphasized the fact that she hated everything Germany was doing and would oppose it with all her strength. Nevertheless, she would resign from the P.E.N. if any majority decision to intervene in any such situation was "forced upon the minority." It was somewhat reminiscent of the occasion, ten years earlier, when the American Center faced a policy decision in connection with Bulgaria, and the Secretary wrote the President, "Should we follow Calvin Coolidge's usual policy and since we don't know just what to do, do nothing?"

When the United States entered the war, some of this confusion disappeared. It was at least clear by now that there was a common enemy and that all Americans had a common goal. It was still not clear, however, what the P.E.N. could do to make itself useful, and less than a month after Pearl Harbor the American Center sent out another questionnaire. There were various spaces to fill out, but the key question was the following: "Have you any suggestions as to ways in which the P.E.N. can work for defense, things you would like to see the P.E.N. do in this crisis?"

The majority left this space blank, and many of the rest filled it in with a simple *no*. One member noted, "I still feel too much in need of guidance myself to offer suggestions to others," and an editor explained why he had not filled out any of the spaces. "My time these days seems to be equally divided between answering questionnaires and making out questionnaires for other people to answer." Most of the members who answered the question offered whatever it was that they themselves wanted for the world, whether it was racial equality or a workable substitute for the League of Nations. And a few, possibly writing at two in the morning, seized the opportunity to

insult their fellow members or other organizations, so blithely
unconscious of misbehavior that they were quite willing to sign
their names.

The same questionnaire was sent to refugee writers, who, as
members of European Centers, were considered associate members of the American P.E.N. Their answers were much more
specific. One writer, "arrested *because* I had been chairman of
the Austrian P.E.N. Club," underwent in the concentration camp
at Dachau an intensive education on the subject of Nazism, and
he suggested that people like himself might visit the army camps
to explain to the soldiers why the United States was in the war.
Another suggested some kind of ceremony on the tenth of May,
"the day of the burning of the books in Germany," and another,
who was "working very hard as a packer and porter," asked if
there was some other way his skills might be used. "With 20
books and several millions of words [of] newspaper publicity
on my record I dreamed of other possibilities in America."

The chairman of what the American Center called its Defense
Committee was a very devoted and hard-working member, Rita
Halle Kleeman, who acted in liaison with Washington and was
able to see that some of the suggestions were used. On the tenth
of May, for instance, the day of the book-burning, a "Freedom
of Books Day" was celebrated and the program included a radio
script written by Stephen Vincent Benét. By this time, however,
the Writers' War Board had been organized as a clearing house
between the writers and the government and had taken over
most of the work that the American Center was trying to do in
this area. The P.E.N. therefore "merged" with this organization,
and Mrs. Kleeman was P.E.N.'s representative on it.

What was never solved was the basic question of the Center's
responsibility for refugee writers. In 1940, it had managed to
send some money to the English and French Centers to help
them in their struggle with the first wave of refugees. But the
American P.E.N. had no machinery to cope with the frantic
pleas for visas, and no money to help support the more fortunate
individuals who were finally able to arrive.

Bessie Beatty resigned in the autumn of 1940 from the dual
post she had been holding as Secretary and Treasurer, although

she still remained on the Board. No P.E.N. member could be found to take on as a volunteer the work she had been doing, and a paid secretary, Jane Hudson, was hired at fifteen dollars a week. Her job was to run the dinners, keep up the correspondence with the members and with the other Centers, and do what she could with all the requests that came to her for help.

Jane Hudson was a remarkable secretary, and she was able to maintain the continuity of kindness that Bessie Beatty had set in motion. But she struggled with an almost insuperable problem; there was no office and almost no funds, and all she could do was to collaborate with other organizations and improvise as she went along. A few faithful members supported her, but the American Center had no machinery to do what it should and no clear path to follow.

This sense of confusion can be illustrated by the dinner which was given by the American Center in the autumn of 1942. The P.E.N. had been founded in London twenty-one years before, and Hermon Ould suggested that the American Center might like to celebrate the coming-of-age of the organization with an appropriate ceremony. "The occasion provides a splendid opportunity for the expression of solidarity among the intellectuals in times of strife and disorder."

In response to this idea, the American Center made plans for an October dinner at the Ambassador Hotel. (These dinners had been going on as before, except that the price had crept up to $2.75 and dress was now informal.) Henry Seidel Canby agreed to give a backward look over the Center's history, and two delegates from the Writers' War Board were asked to be present, to "tell us how, in their opinion, the writer should slant his work during the present crisis."

The dinner, planned so carefully, was nearly a disaster. For the two speakers from the Writers' War Board made it passionately clear that the duty of writers was to hate not only the Nazis but the whole of the German nation.

This was what the English Center had specifically warned against: "A writer who persuades us to hate is ensuring that we are unfit to make peace. One of his tasks is to keep us sane." This principle had by now been subjected to almost intolerable

strain, but it was still true, and many writers still knew it. When
the American Center sent out its questionnaire a few months
earlier, asking what the organization ought to be doing, one of
the answers was: "Keep before the public the fact that hating
doesn't win wars."

Some of the P.E.N. members at the Ambassador dinner were
instantly on their feet to reject the doctrine of wholesale hate
they had just been offered. Chief among them were Canby himself, Will Irwin, Norman Cousins and Arthur Garfield Hays, all
expressing their determined opposition to what seemed to them
a horrifying position. Both sides began shouting and banging
their fists on the table, and as soon as the President could obtain
a moment of comparative quiet he hastily declared the meeting
adjourned.

The American P.E.N. got more publicity than it wanted out
of the battle, including a full page in the *Saturday Review of
Literature* with sketches of some of the combatants. In the
annual report of the Center, what had originally been called
a "heated and even tumultuous" battle was described instead
as a meeting "fruitful in discussion and argument." It was
hardly that. Even less had it been the "expression of solidarity"
for which Hermon Ould had been hoping. It did, however,
illustrate how difficult it was for American writers to reach
agreement.

Jane Hudson and a faithful few did their best all through the
war years. Small sums of money were raised and applied where
they would do the most good. Every effort was made, working
with other organizations, to help with visas, affidavits and costs
of transportation for refugees and to help them find jobs after
they arrived in the United States. But nearly every member was
already working individually to do what he could, and there was
no way for the Center to mount a really concerted and sustained
effort.

Perhaps the greatest casualty of this period was the loss of an
adequate relationship between the New York Center and the
parent organization in London. It had been weakening for some
time and, as Ould remarked gently at the end of the 1930's, the
fact that the Americans had not been sending anyone to repre-

sent them at the meetings of the International Executive Committee might account in part for "a certain vagueness in the States concerning the aims and constitution of the P.E.N."

The most depressing example of the failure of this relationship occurred in 1941, on the occasion of the International Congress that was held in London. This was an event of great symbolic importance, taking place as it did in time of war, but the American Center sent no delegates and the membership was not even informed that the Congress was taking place. It seemed so vital from the international point of view that the United States should be represented that the English government supplied a plane to bring two American writers, John Dos Passos and Thornton Wilder, to the P.E.N. Congress. Wilder was not at the moment a member of the American Center, having let his membership lapse, and he was hurriedly asked to rejoin after his return.

In spite of good will and good intentions, the American Center was clearly in difficulties, and in March of 1943 it was decided to have a reorganization. Three Vice-Presidents were created, which was a new office in the history of the Center. Everyone on the Board resigned, and the Nominating Committee was empowered to reconsider the whole question of Board membership.

As the retiring President remarked, "The President of the P.E.N. doesn't have an easy job," but the incoming President embarked on his duties hopefully. He was determined to make the Center "a more effective and dynamic organization," and he set up a large number of committees whose members were carefully chosen. Bessie Beatty, for instance, was asked to serve on the foreign affairs committee, and Walter White on domestic affairs. The most reluctant, naturally, were those who were asked to serve on the finance committee, but the replies to the President's letter of request were cordial. As one member put it, "I can't say no to anything you ask me to do."

There was even a special committee whose responsibility was to issue a pamphlet which would give a history of the organization. This was an old dream; back in 1928, the Secretary noted,

"We have considered for a long time past having a pamphlet describing the P.E.N." Bessie Beatty told Hermon Ould in 1939, "We have long felt the need here of just such a document for general circulation, and especially for the new members." Now, at last, it seemed possible that it would really come into being, and the chairman of the Publications Committee was so enthusiastic about the idea that in June of 1944 he offered to pay a hundred dollars toward expenses.

At the same time, a real effort was made to strengthen the links that bound the Club to the other Centers, and during this same summer letters were addressed to every P.E.N. Center in the world. The plan was to hold a special dinner in November of 1944, to symbolize the importance of the P.E.N. and to discuss its function in the post-war world. Each Center was asked to send a representative to the dinner, if that was possible, or at least to send a message.

Two months before the date of the dinner, Paris was liberated and the French Center was able to reopen. Its records had been systematically destroyed, its headquarters stripped and occupied by the Gestapo, and nothing remained of the *Maison Internationale* except a few chairs in a single room. It was all the more a meeting place of the spirit, and among those who gathered there were "Paul Valéry, Georges Duhamel, Henri Membré, Vercours. . . ." Membré was Secretary of the French Center, and Arthur Koestler owed his life to him when he took refuge in Paris. Then Membré himself had been forced to flee the city, but now he was back again, ready to take up the rebuilding of all that had been destroyed.

The American Center held its gala dinner on the 15th of November, and there were letters from thirteen Centers to be read. There was an extremely large and enthusiastic attendance and everything went off elegantly, and yet the occasion was not really a success. The bitterness and confusion of the war were still tragically in evidence, and a very distinguished French writer who had accepted an invitation to be one of the speakers was suddenly informed that he would not be welcome at the dinner because there had been protests against his presence.

The English Center was represented at the dinner by Somerset Maugham, chiefly because he was the only prominent English writer who happened to be in the United States at the moment. Ould himself had suggested him, and Maugham gave a brief and rather clever speech. His contribution to the basic idea of the evening was not, however, a particularly useful one. "I have been asked what the P.E.N. Club will do most effectively after the war. I think what it can most effectively do is to do nothing."

When Hermon Ould read the speech, he remarked, "I find Mr. Somerset Maugham's pessimism a little disconcerting." The International Secretary was not really disconcerted, however. He merely ignored the pessimism as irrelevant, since it was clear that Maugham knew nothing whatever about the P.E.N.

There were others who saw its function more clearly. Storm Jameson was in ravaged Poland immediately after the war, and she met an old man who had been a professor at Cracow University. He and his fellow teachers at the University had been sent to a concentration camp, and out of the hundred and thirty he was the only one who survived. "I will show you my dear possession," he told Storm Jameson, and he brought out of his pocket his membership card in the International P.E.N.

The American Center was one of the very few that had not suffered during the war, and it was perhaps partly on that account that it faced the post-war period in such a confused state of mind. It needed a clear focus for its activities, something to which its members could respond whole-heartedly and without reservations. It was here, once more, that Henry Seidel Canby did the Center a great service, for he suggested "a post-war project to aid foreign writers" and was at once made chairman of a special committee.

The original intention of this committee was to obtain reliable lists of European writers who were in need and then to try to get a grant to finance the sending of relief packages. But, by the summer of 1945, the three working members of the committee gave up this idea; it was much more difficult than they had foreseen to get reliable lists and the need was much more urgent. Therefore they divided the work: Ben Huebsch

loaned enough money to get the thing started, Robert Pick
concentrated on the lists, and Manuel Komroff started the
packages on their way.

Each package went to an individual writer with a letter ex-
plaining that it was a gift of love and homage from fellow writers
in America; it was a gift of the spirit, and the recipients took it
as such. A Hungarian wrote: "I am very proud that it is not
from an American relative or a rich friend, but from the writers
of America. . . . Even if it is addressed to me, it is actually
meant for the Hungarian literature, for our old Europe and for
the idea of human solidarity." A Greek writer said: "This
morning I received your valuable packet of affection . . . the
only expression of love and affection since our liberation." And,
from Vienna: "A poet today seems to have no right to exist at
all. But things may turn for the better. Is not your parcel a
sign?"

The packages did not always reach their destination in perfect condition. In the early days, before CARE had been organized and could take over the actual sending, the bouillon cubes
might arrive enveloped in honey, or the bottom of the box
might turn out to be covered by "a peaceful mixture of lentils,
tea, coffee, barley." But this was a minor matter. What was
important to the recipients was what one of them called "this
expression of love . . . this present of love," and the sense it gave
of faith in the future. As another writer put it, the package
"was not only a great help to me to continue my work, but
much more than that: it was encouragement and moral trust. . . .
My colleagues have been killed because they were not willing to
be servant-minded, because they loved freedom and they
behaved as men." The writer himself had been wounded by a
German bullet but had survived. "I am living! I have got my pen
again in my hands. I am working!"*

---

*There was also a Special Gifts Committee which sent whatever clothing it could
gather together, and again the writers of Europe sent their gratitude. The chairman
of this committee wrote the President of the American Center: "Would you like a
book on French Philosophy from an old member of the Academy in appreciation of
the blanket? He wants to send one. I hate to let him waste postage, but think it would
be polite to accept. He is over eighty and bedridden and loves the blanket."

The members of the American Center responded with real ardor to the request for contributions, grateful to be given something specific to do. Some of them encountered delays in getting the money to New York. One member who was living in Tahiti was late in hearing of the idea, since, as he said, "steamers to our part of the Pacific are few and far between." He hurried a bank note by air to New York via Bora Bora and only regretted that "I cannot send ten times the sum."

In the end, the committee raised $17,777.77 from the membership and sent 1223 packages to twelve countries, always with a letter addressed to a writer who loved freedom and who had not been "servant-minded." Thomas Mann, writing to the American Center in 1949, noted that the packages had been deeply appreciated "both for their actual and spiritual value," and it was this affirmation of the things of the spirit which explains the willingness of the Center to work with energy and grace once it had been given a specific task to perform.

In 1946 there was a second achievement, for the pamphlet history which had been planned two years earlier at last became a reality. The delay had been caused, at least in part, by the fact that it was very difficult to get the necessary information together. The American Center had never had a headquarters of its own, and each Secretary was supposed to hold the files during his term of office and then pass them on to his successor. One of them noted ruefully, "The early archives of P.E.N. were lost sometime after I turned them over to my successor as Secretary in 1929." When a letter of inquiry arrived in 1932, asking for the constitution of the Center, there was only one possible answer: "The New York Center has no constitution. From all the records which were handed over to me, the club seems to have no constitution, no bylaws and no history."

Not only was it nearly impossible to unearth early material for the proposed P.E.N. history, but no one wanted to do the actual writing. Another committee was set up to struggle with this problem, and a rough draft was worked out which was finished by Will Irwin and to which he put his name. The result was a neatly printed little booklet, which contained the names and addresses of all the American members, the names of the

foreign Centers with their Secretaries, and an eleven-page history
of the P.E.N. There were inevitably a few errors, especially in
the matter of dates, but it was a lively and well-written little
story and the first indication to most of the members of what
the history of the organization had been. Above all, it emphasized the international character of P.E.N., and the last page
noted that "the first International Congress of the post-war
period will meet at Stockholm in the summer of 1946."

This was the Congress that had been planned for the autumn
of 1939 and which had been made impossible by the outbreak
of the war. Hermon Ould refused to believe that it would not
ultimately take place. He was sure that it was Hitlerism that
would be destroyed and not the P.E.N. Driven from London
in 1942, he decided that this was the proper time to reprint
the P.E.N. rules, "adding the texts of the important and binding
'Canby' and 'Raymond' resolutions. . . . This reprinting of the
Rules now, while the war is raging, will give officials of the P.E.N.
Centers all over the world an opportunity of examining them in
moments of leisure."*

Ould's steadfast faith was justified. The Congress was held
triumphantly at Stockholm in 1946, when the lilacs were in
bloom, and members who had believed each other dead were
able to meet again. An old professor of Finland had been working on his speech all through the war, as confident as Hermon Ould
that it would eventually be possible to deliver it, and he read it
with hands that trembled as they held the papers.

It was a tumultuous Congress, for the writers of Europe inevitably split up into nationalistic patterns and waved rival banners,
but its very tumult showed that P.E.N. was unmistakably alive.
In fact, as Ould pointed out, "It is one of the few international

---

*The Canby resolution was the one that had been unanimously passed at the
Dubrovnik Congress of 1933 and which incorporated the three articles passed at
Brussels in 1927. The Raymond resolution had been passed in the Edinburgh Congress of 1934 and was a general condemnation of censorship: "The P.E.N. stands for
liberty of expression throughout the world and views with apprehension the continual
attempts to encroach upon that liberty in the name of social security and international
strategy. It affirms its belief that the necessary advance of the world towards a more
highly organized political and economic order renders a free criticism of administrations
and institutions imperative from all points of view."

societies which has not only survived but has increased its scope during the world war."

Ould was extremely anxious to have a good showing from the American Center, and Jane Hudson struggled gamely with the problem. The difficulty, as usual, was money. The Center could pay two hundred and fifty dollars toward the delegate's expenses, which was not nearly enough, and a friend in Sweden wrote urgently in April: "Prince Wilhelm, president of the Swedish P.E.N. Club . . . approached us rather despairingly about American representation. . . . I cannot stress the importance of the matter enough."

It was Henry Goddard Leach who finally agreed to be the American delegate to Stockholm, and, as he pointed out, it was hardly a new problem. "In 1928 I was the only American delegate to the P.E.N. Congress at Oslo." Marc Connelly also agreed to go, since he was in London and did not have far to travel, and one more difficulty was surmounted.

Moreover, the American delegation brought with it an invitation to hold a Congress in New York in 1948. Ould had pointed out that a meeting in the United States "would immensely enhance the prestige and effectiveness of the P.E.N." and certainly the event was long overdue. The only official Congress in New York had been held in 1924. The invitation was received with enthusiasm at Stockholm in 1946, and it was one of the few items on the long and crowded agenda on which there was general agreement.

Leach also brought with him two resolutions. These were backed by the English Center and debated on the fifth of June. One of them merely called on members of the P.E.N. to "champion the ideals of one humanity living at peace in one world," but the other was a specific attack on the problem of censorship.

> So far as is consistent with public order and accepted national standards of decency, we declare for a free press and oppose arbitrary censorship in time of peace. And since freedom implies voluntary restraint . . . we pledge ourselves to oppose such evils of a free press as mendacious publication, deliberate falsehood and distortion of facts for political and personal ends. Members of the P.E.N. are pledged to active and public protest

against any form of suppression of freedom of expression in
the country and community to which they belong.

The French and Belgian delegations objected vigorously to the
wording of the opening sentence, since nearly all political censorship is imposed in the name of "public order." The majority
of the delegates agreed with them, and it was voted to omit the
offending phrase.

The next Congress was held in Zurich in 1947, and what was
called the "American Resolution" was still being argued. Censorship was an extremely complicated subject, and the American
Center was fortunate to have as one of its delegates that year
a playwright who took a passionate and informed interest in the
problem. Elmer Rice had not been very interested in P.E.N.
in its early days, except that he had attended a dinner on censorship in 1930; when he joined the American Center nine years
later, he said he had so little extra time at his disposal that he
could not be very helpful. "But I'll do what I can." Rice was
invaluable at the Zurich Congress, and with his help the resolution on censorship was once more rewritten.

The other American delegate at Zurich in 1947 was Ben
Huebsch, who had already performed many services for the
American Center. He reaffirmed the invitation to hold the next
year's Congress in New York, and this was received "with accla-
mation." Both he and Rice, however, sent home warnings that
heavy currency restrictions were in force all over Europe. It was
going to be very difficult to get adequate representation unless
the American Center was willing to pay travel expenses.

It was in 1946 that the Board had made the decision to hold
the 1948 Congress in New York, and this happened to be a year
in which things looked very hopeful for the American Center.
There had been great activity with the food packages, the pamphlet on P.E.N. history had just been issued, and the raising of
the dues to ten dollars had put the Club on a better financial
basis. It was true that a dinner which had been planned in
honor of the United Nations had to be cancelled "because of
the lack of response from the membership," but this only
showed how much an International Congress was needed.
Above all, Bessie Beatty had agreed to serve as chairman of the

planning committee, and she was the one who had guided the World's Fair Congress to its successful conclusion.

Early in 1947, Bessie Beatty died. When the Board met in April, another P.E.N. member agreed to serve as "temporary chairman," and he embarked on his task with enthusiasm and hopefulness. Eighteen committees were set up, the Waldorf Astoria was chosen as convention headquarters and, by May, negotiations with its Banquet Department had been started. A theme was chosen for the Congress—"What is the Machine Age Doing to Culture?"—and it was hoped that the subject would interest many allied organizations. By August, the original budget of twenty thousand dollars had climbed to sixty thousand and the Congress itself was still a year away.

As soon as the original invitation was confirmed at the Zurich Congress in June of 1947, the European Centers began to send enthusiastic letters with hopeful inquiries that were very hard to answer. It was clear that the Americans were not going to be able to pay the transportation of the foreign delegates, as was so obviously expected. It was also increasingly clear that no Congress of any kind could be financed unless the American Center managed to get tax exemption.

A year earlier, this battle for tax exemption had been fought on a much more limited terrain. The Book-of-the-Month Club had offered to contribute five thousand dollars toward the fund for relief packages if the gift was tax exempt, and all early efforts in this direction failed. Finally that good friend of the P.E.N., Frederic Melcher, went down to Washington with a lawyer. Thanks to an intervention on their behalf by the Under Secretary of State, Melcher and the lawyer were able to sit in the Internal Revenue Office while a fleet of secretaries brought them the necessary papers to sign. On the same day in which tax exemption was thus achieved, the Internal Revenue mailed a formal notice to the American Center that its request for tax exemption had been turned down, which was a classic example of the right hand not knowing what the left hand had been doing.

This tax exemption of 1946 was a very limited one; it applied only to contributions to the fund for packages to Europe. It

proved impossible, the following year, to persuade the Internal
Revenue Office that the American Center of P.E.N. ought itself
to be a tax-exempt organization, and it was equally impossible
to collect contributions for the forthcoming Congress when tax
exemption was lacking. The European Centers passed the summer of 1947 confidently expecting a wonderful Congress in
1948 in rich America, while the worried Americans became increasingly sure that there was not going to be enough money for
any kind of a Congress at all.

The "temporary chairman" was abroad in the early autumn,
and when he returned in October he made a very pessimistic
report to the Board. It was almost impossible to take money
out of Europe, and the expenses of most of the delegates would
therefore have to be underwritten. This was clearly impossible,
and the Board voted to withdraw the invitation.

The news came as a "great shock" to the Europeans, since the
cancellation was both sudden and unexpected. For a time, it
seemed that there would be no P.E.N. Congress in 1948. Then
the Danes, who had been planning for a Congress in 1950,
offered to set the date back two years. This gave them very
little time to make their preparations, but they managed nevertheless to produce a very successful Congress in Copenhagen.

This Congress of 1948 was of the greatest importance, for it
was here, in Copenhagen, that the P.E.N. Charter at last came
into being. It consisted of the three articles that had been approved at Brussels in 1927 and reinforced at Dubrovnik in 1933,
and of a fourth article which put into final form the statement
on censorship that had been discussed in so many Congresses.*

This was the rock that was to support the P.E.N. in so many
later periods of stress, for, as Ould said cheerfully, "So long as
we stick to our charter we can't go far wrong." From that time
forward, the Charter was the central reality of the P.E.N., and
it proved durable precisely because it had been built so slowly
and tested by so many conflicting opinions.

It was also at this Congress of 1948 that the German and the
Japanese Centers came back into existence, now once more will-

---

*See the Appendix for the full text of the Charter.

ing to "champion the ideals of one humanity living at peace in one world."

The delegates from the American Center brought with them an official letter, which had been written and rewritten, to explain that "money restrictions" had made it necessary for the Center to withdraw its invitation. Almost no one at the Congress believed this explanation. The general opinion was that the cancellation had been political and that the Americans had been either unwilling or unable to welcome "Poles, Czechs and others under Russian domination." Or, as *The New York Times* put it, "The political standing of some of the leading delegates had made it seem unlikely that they would be permitted to enter the United States."

There was some truth in this. But it was equally true, and even more to the point, that the gulf between the American Center and International P.E.N. had been widening. Men like Prince Wilhelm of Sweden and Hermon Ould had made every effort to draw the American Center into the work of the International, but most Americans had relatively little knowledge of what went on abroad and cared less.

The planners of the ill-fated New York Congress knew very little about the P.E.N. as a whole. They announced firmly that the P in the name stood for publishers as well as for playwrights and poets, and Ould was obliged to write and explain that it did not. They called the forthcoming event "the 13th Congress," when it was, in fact, the twentieth. It came as a surprise to one of these planners that there was supposed to be a record of the proceedings—"I did not dream that the speeches might be printed"—and equally a surprise to find that the American Center was supposed to send a delegate to the meetings of the International Executive Committee.

All this reflected a profound ignorance of the nature of the tree of which the American Center was one of the branches, and a perhaps equally profound conviction that it really did not matter very much after all. The Congress was put aside as something better forgotten, and nothing remained of all the hopeful dreams and the hard work except the seal that had been designed for the occasion. It showed within an oval a triumphant pen and a

broken sword, very gracefully designed, and this emblem was
used on the stationery from that time forward.

The Board which had met in October of 1947 and voted to
cancel the Congress held a long discussion at this same meeting
of what other ways there might be to make the organization
"significant." There was talk of a membership drive; articles
and radio programs might be planned; a newsletter was a possibility; perhaps also there might be "monthly teas for our own
members." The social activities for the whole of that year
consisted of three dinners, one lunch and one tea, and the committee on European relief was the only committee extant out of all
the "elaborate series" that had been set up two years earlier.

This was the one area in which the American Center was sure
of itself and what it could do. Two years later, for instance, an
appeal was sent to all the P.E.N. Centers from the President of
the Polish Center, Jan Parandowski. He asked for help in repla-
cing the Center's collection of foreign books, burned by the
Nazi invaders, and he offered Polish books in exchange. The
American Center promptly asked thirty publishers to donate
books, and the Slavonic Division of The New York Public
Library assumed the responsibility for shipping them overseas.
When Parandowski saw his colleagues at the Congress in Venice
that summer, he thanked them for their contributions. Yet
he felt that the American Center should have been thanked
twice over, for they had sent more books than any other and
all of them in perfect condition.

The American Center was capable of acting with energy and
imagination when there was a clear need, but most of the time
it seemed to be only drifting. Committees were set up but they
held no meetings. Plans were made and they came to nothing.
In 1948, Canby agreed to serve as President, since no one else
could be found. But he made it clear that he would be only a
name on the stationery, since he could not be in New York, and
a Presidential Committee was set up to take his place.

The occasional successes continued. A very knowledgeable
individual agreed to represent the American Center at the meeting of the International Executive early in 1949; he was already
in London. That same year, John Dos Passos agreed to be a dele-

gate to the Congress in Venice, but the problem of financing the trip was matched by the reluctance of the delegate himself. "I have the gravest misgivings about my usefulness in an operation of this kind, and shall feel only relief if you change your minds." The following year the Congress was held in Edinburgh, and the delegation from the American Center was the same size as the one from Estonia.

Back in 1946, Jane Hudson had talked of resigning her post as secretary and had been persuaded to stay on. Three years later, she wrote to thank Rita Kleeman for her "unfailing and constant help," which had not faltered throughout the whole of the decade. There were perhaps a dozen other members who had shown the same sense of responsibility; they could help keep the Club in existence but they could not give it a sense of direction.

In the summer of 1950, Jane Hudson decided definitely to resign, the resignation to take effect at the end of the year. Ten years earlier, Klaus Mann had "watched a lively something in red, rushing around and announcing on her frontside that she was the new secretary of the P.E.N. Club," and ever since she had been its chief support and its willing, kindhearted, energetic center. It seemed hard to believe that the organization, already faltering, could survive without her.

One especially perturbed member was Frederic Melcher, who had been a faithful friend to the P.E.N. ever since the days, more than a quarter of a century ago, when he had helped to make the arrangements for the New York Congress of 1924. When he heard the "bad news" that Jane Hudson was leaving, he wrote her a long letter.

> I am rather at a loss to know what to say. It always seems as though a new era of strength and extended usefulness for P.E.N. is always just around the corner. I think the purposes of P.E.N. have always been important and now are extremely important. If I didn't think so I certainly wouldn't take as seriously the many committees and social meetings. . . . I do have a sense of values on things that affect books and I know such an organization as this is important.

He added that most American writers thought that the activities of the Center were only "side issues from their real interest of writing. The importance of P.E.N. doesn't come home to them here as it does in Europe."

In June of 1950, a Steering Committee had been set up to discuss possible ways of revitalizing the Center. All the old dreams had been talked over—such as raising money for a headquarters, giving awards to writers and so on—and out of this came plans for yet another committee. This would be a small one, whose members would really work together, and that summer Melcher sat on Jane Hudson's porch at Cape Cod to discuss possible members for this committee. Canby was asked to serve as chairman and refused. "I am deeply engaged on a much delayed book." Nearly everyone was hoping against hope that Jane Hudson might remain. But she could not, and a new secretary took her place.

In May of 1951, the time had come for the election of new officers. It was the custom for the outgoing Secretary to present a report which summarized the activities of the past year. The current Secretary had held the post since 1947 and had served the P.E.N. faithfully in many other ways. Since he valued the organization, he decided to tell the truth. Instead of a polite report on the past year, he composed a vigorous and honest statement describing the present weakness of the American Center. "Our most serious problem is the lack of interest and lack of activity." Only thirty members had been present at the last dinner, and most of the Board members did not come to its meetings. "Another year or two of inactivity and we will lose the last remnants of our creative writers. Because of the importance of the problem this report has included little else."

Back in 1939, Hermon Ould was already worried about the vitality of the American P.E.N. and had suggested hopefully that perhaps the enthusiasm generated by the success of the World's Fair Congress would be "a safeguard against the demise of your centre." The American Center had struggled through the next decade without dying, but neither, precisely, had it lived. There had been occasional moments of triumph, but in general all that it had managed to do was to stay in existence.

Part Three

Hermon Ould died in September of 1951. He had no special reason to believe that the American Center would survive very much longer. Nevertheless, his faith in the P.E.N. was indomitable and unquestionably he was convinced that the American Center would recover its energy and its sense of direction.

In fact, this process had already begun.

What had occurred was something that happened frequently in the American Center, and still does. An individual member, sometimes one who has been inactive for a long time, suddenly finds his imagination roused by a specific problem and is altogether willing to shoulder the responsibilities that go with it. There have been many such men and women in the history of the Center; the one who was visited early in the 1950's by this odd, bright vision was John Farrar.

Three decades earlier, Farrar had worked hard for the American Center. He had helped to organize it, he arranged its first dinner meeting at the Coffee House Club, and he was one of the planners of the New York Congress of 1924. Then the redheaded young editor of *The Bookman* went into publishing, and the Center saw relatively little of him until 1949.

In that year, Farrar became chairman of the Admissions Committee. The admission of new members had always been handled with care and intelligence by the American Center, but there had never been anything like the sudden vigor shown by the new chairman. In May of 1950, when the annual business meeting was held at a thinly attended luncheon in the New Weston Hotel, there was the usual lack of activity to report, but this time there was a single exception: "The admissions committee has done an admirable job this year." It had indeed. The previous year, twenty new members had entered the American Center; this year there were ninety-seven.

In the following spring, that of 1951, the outgoing Secretary composed the report in which he described unsparingly the weaknesses of the American Center. In the course of it he noted: "Much ground has been lost. But there is still a chance that the illness may find a cure." In this he was correct; for Farrar, who had been serving that year as Treasurer, suddenly decided that he was willing to be President.

The Secretary's report was never read to the membership, for the new President was in no mood to look backward or to regret the past. He went to work with the same enthusiasm he had shown two years earlier when he was gathering in new members, and in fact he was a kind of whirlwind, upsetting some of the members by the amount of dust he raised and delighting others whose desire for action was as strong as his own.

Inevitably, like any new President, he formed a great many committees. This was the usual procedure, and in many cases they had been stillborn. But Farrar watched over his committees like a mother hen, attending all the meetings, urging on his hand-picked chairmen, and keeping them hard at work all through the summer of 1951. This in itself was unusual, since the summer was traditionally a time for hibernation for the P.E.N.

Anyone who had shown the least interest in the Center was likely to be commandeered for service. One member had sent in a bitter letter denouncing the Center's weakness from the international point of view, and he was promptly asked "to be co-chairman of a committee on the development of our international position." The distinguished member failed to answer the letter that contained this invitation—it being far easier to criticize a situation than to help change it—and the new President started down a different avenue to improve the Center's relationship to the rest of the world. In fact, he was quite capable of starting down a dozen avenues, being cheerfully convinced that if one method did not work another probably would.

One of the special problems that faced the American P.E.N. was the fact that it had been losing the sense of informal good fellowship that was one of its reasons for existing. During the past decade, a great deal of work and planning had gone into the dinner meetings, but it was difficult to get speakers and becoming increasingly so. This was partly because many of the best writers are congenitally not speakers.* Moreover, unless the writer was well known or very provocative, it was difficult to persuade the membership to come and at least two dinners had to be cancelled for lack of attendance.

Sometimes a single dinner had been a great success. There was, for instance, a dinner in 1945 for Robert Frost, in honor of the poet's seventieth birthday and the publication of his *Masque of Reason*. There was a dinner in 1950 at which Mrs. Roosevelt was the speaker, with an introduction by Robert Sherwood. But, in general, the formal dinners with their place-cards and their carefully arranged tables had become an increasing burden on the devoted few who planned them, and they received little thanks for their efforts. One member suggested darkly in October of 1948, "Perhaps there is a reason for not trying for good speakers."

In the middle of May, 1951, the Executive Committee considered a report "that many younger members . . . have requested that buffet and cocktail parties take the place of formal dinners." John Farrar was still Treasurer when he attended this meeting of the Executive Committee, but as soon as he became President a few weeks later he set about putting the ideas of the younger members into practice.

---

*In 1949, for instance, Jane Hudson wrote to Storm Jameson, "We would be most grateful if you would speak to us for as long as you like on any subject that you like," and received the despairing answer, "I am truly not a speaker. . . . What shall I do? Break my leg on April 12th?" Later in this same year, Jane Hudson tried T. S. Eliot, who was even more appalled. "Your kind letter of October 2nd . . . has caused me much distress and terror. . . . I am very bad at making after-dinner speeches."

Instead of a formal dinner to open the fall season in 1951, there was an informal dinner at the Lotos Club. This buffet cost only two dollars, which was considerably less than the price of the old dinners, and the President asked everyone to come and bring vigorous opinions. It did not seem likely that there would be much discussion, since the program consisted merely of a speech on copyright and a report on the recent P.E.N. Congress in Lausanne. In fact, however, the report turned out to be bitterly controversial, for the American delegation had been persuaded to back a resolution which was Communist-inspired.

The Congress at Lausanne had been held in June and was the last one that Hermon Ould attended before he died. It was a very argumentative Congress, and Ould never objected to controversy. As he said, "Ideas cannot thrive in a vacuum. They thrive, as *all* things thrive, by their ability to hold their own against opposing forces." But he was determined that the P.E.N. should never permit itself to be used by political ideologies, and the resolution that the Americans had innocently backed belonged in this category. The Board of the American Center was of this same opinion and ultimately voted to repudiate the action.

When the report from the American delegation was presented at the Lotos Club, one of the most vigorous protests came from a new member who was in the audience. This was Franz Schoenberner, the former editor of *Simplicissimus* who had been forced into exile because of his hatred of what the Nazis represented. More than most writers, he knew that P.E.N. must never slide into the position of supporting one form of political tyranny because of its hatred for another. "I feel rather strongly about the idea of spiritual freedom, which, for almost forty years, with a rather monotonous consistency, I have defended in three countries and three languages against any kind of dictatorship."*

*Less than two months after this October dinner at the Lotos Club, Schoenberner, having survived three concentration camps, was attacked in the hallway of his apartment building and crippled for life. The American Center raised three thousand dollars for him, and its members were grateful for the opportunity. When he had recovered sufficiently from what had been almost complete paralysis to be able to move one finger, he started typing his third book, and the P.E.N. had the pleasure of sending him an electric typewriter which he tenderly called "this friendly machine."

After the opening evening at the Lotos Club, the P.E.N. moved
to the Town Hall Club with its more central location. The prices
crept up, as prices will, and soon the members were paying as much
for their buffet dinners as under the old system. But they liked
the informality and the lively atmosphere in which controversy
flourished. The chairman of the Activities Committee armed herself with a brass elephant bell from India, and, if anyone exceed-
ed the allotted time, she rang the bell vigorously.

Instead of individual speakers there were now panels, chosen
with the hope that the panelists would disagree with each other.
In January of 1952, a group of editors addressed itself to that
perennial question, "What's Wrong with Writers?" In February,
William Styron and Gore Vidal argued with two other novelists.
In March, Stella Adler, Oscar Hammerstein, Anita Loos and
Arthur Miller discussed the current state of the stage (this one
was held at the Harkness Theatre), and in April, now back at
the Town Hall Club, there was a discussion of "Psychoanalysis
and the Writer."

In May came the business meeting and the election of officers.
Normally this annual event was a poorly attended luncheon but
this year it was a crowded buffet dinner. In fact, all the dinners
that season had been well attended. Attendance "varied between
61 and 112," which was an unprecedented figure to maintain
month after month.

The other form of social activity which the younger members
had suggested was the giving of cocktail parties. An occasional
meeting of this kind had been held over the years, usually in the
home of a member when there was some special guest from
abroad. In May of 1950, however, there had been a cocktail
party at Rockefeller Center to honor any member who had
recently published a book, with another one the following March.
In both cases an advance reservation had to be made and there
was a charge of a dollar to cover the cost of one drink. The Treasurer's report for the season that ended in the spring of 1951 had
listed "two cocktail parties, two dinners and one business lunch."

The following year, there were not only eight dinners but
twenty-six cocktail parties to report. "Each gathering honored
one or two guests, either important American authors for their

recent books, or distinguished guests and members from abroad.
We were especially fortunate . . . in having the opportunity to
entertain so many of our colleagues from other Centers, representing countries in Asia, Europe and South America as well as
other American cities." Most of these afternoon receptions
were held at the Algonquin Hotel, and the idea of requesting
reservations was scrapped. Everyone except the guests of honor
paid for his own drinks, and the emphasis was on informality
and good fellowship.

Of all the innovations that were introduced in 1951, this was
one of the most valuable. It supplied a pleasant and neutral
meeting place where writers and editors from all over the world
could encounter each other casually without any complications.
The chief problem in the early days was to find a satisfactory
place to meet, and the American Center tried in turn the New
Weston, the Algonquin, the Waldorf Astoria, the Sherry-Netherland and the Ambassador hotels. Finally, in 1955, it settled
down at the Hotel Pierre and it has been there ever since.

These gatherings are usually called cocktail parties, although
the Pierre calls them P.E.N. receptions and perhaps that is a
better word. Although the area around the bar is always crowded,
some of the members and their guests do not drink at all, some
carry about a glass of gingerale, and on one occasion the Pierre
even managed to produce, heroically, a cup of tea for a guest of
honor at his request. No one is expected to be sociable unless
he feels like it; he can greet everyone, strangers included, if he
wishes, or he can sit peacefully in a chair and eat peanuts. In
the early days, the guests of honor were identified by the wearing of a paper clip—both to ensure them the two free drinks that
were their due and to make it possible for their fellow writers
to identify them. Later, as the American Center grew more
prosperous, the paper clips became small sprigs of green and now
they are likely to be carnations or button chrysanthemums.

Sometimes the parties at the Pierre are very large ones. This
usually occurs if the guests of honor are especially well known
or when, as happens once a year, they are the out-of-town book
reviewers who have come to New York for the National Book
Awards. Sometimes the parties have been relatively small and

for that reason even more sociable. The smallest ever held was
on a winter afternoon when a very heavy snowstorm paralyzed
the city and all surface transportation ceased. Every reservation
that had been made with the Pierre was cancelled, excepting
only the one made by the P.E.N. About a dozen members managed to mush their way through the drifts and so did at least
one of the guests of honor; and no one was more proud than
the bartender, who by this time was taking a proprietary interest
in the gatherings after so long and friendly a relationship.

One of the special advantages of these afternoon parties was
that they so clearly strengthened the international side of the
P.E.N. They made it easy for American writers to meet a
Danish publisher or a Japanese novelist or an African poet, sometimes with the aid of an interpreter but usually through a smat-
tering of each other's languages and much good will. Occasionally the foreign writers came in groups. There was more than
one literary delegation from Russia; in 1959 a group of seven
young writers from abroad included a novelist who was almost
unknown at the time—Günter Grass. These were men and women
whom the American membership would not normally have met,
and the State Department made it clear how much it appreciated
"all that P.E.N. has done . . . for so many of our visiting writers
and journalists from abroad. . . . We are more grateful than I
can say."

It was an excellent thing to be able to welcome visiting authors
and editors from abroad, but it was even more important for
the American Center to take up again its direct obligations to
International P.E.N. This was a relationship which had become
erratic and, in one or two cases, irresponsible, and it was of the
utmost importance that the machinery which had grown rusty
with disuse should begin to function again.

The chief difficulty, of course, was money. The meetings of
the International Executive Committee and the Congresses
themselves were almost always held in Europe, and Europe was
a long way off. As the Secretary of the American Center noted
mournfully in 1946: 'For American writers to get there is so
expensive, it is prohibitive." The membership dues barely paid
for current expenses and could not be raised substantially since

some of the best writers in the United States make the least
money. As a result, since there was no way to pay travel expenses, the representative from the American Center was frequently
someone who was planning to go abroad in any case and who
knew almost nothing about the P.E.N.

The problem was constantly discussed at Board meetings,
and various foundations were approached, always without success. Finally, in May of 1954, a letter was sent to the Board of
Directors of the Farfield Foundation, a small foundation which
concerned itself with international affairs. The letter explained
that the American Center wanted to send a delegate to the
forthcoming P.E.N. Congress in Amsterdam, and it asked the
Foundation for $558, which was the cost of a round-trip tourist
flight. The check arrived six days later. From that time forward,
the Farfield Foundation showed itself willing to pay the traveling expenses of the official Congress delegates from the American
Center, and the single greatest obstacle to the Center's responsible
behavior as a branch of International P.E.N. was removed.

The following month the Secretary made his annual report
to the membership and noted: "On the whole, the American
Center would seem to be in a very healthy state, and we hope
to maintain the ground which we have gained in the last two or
three years." A new President was taking over, since Farrar's
term of office had run its course under the bylaws that had
been written in 1951, but he and all subsequent Presidents kept
up the momentum that had now been established.

The dinners continued to be as lively as ever. Some of them
were well attended and some were not, but the room at the
Town Hall Club was flexible enough to accommodate a very large
crowd or a small one. There was, predictably, a large attendance
when Norman Mailer and Georges Simenon discussed the subject of "Sex in Literature." There was also a large turnout the
following year when a group of distinguished historians—Bruce
Catton, Allan Nevins and C. V. Wedgwood as speakers and James
Thomas Flexner as moderator—gathered to celebrate the first
issue of *American Heritage.*

In April of 1955, the American Center joined with the America-
Italy Society to give a dinner for Alberto Moravia in the Grand Ball-

room of the Park-Sheraton. The guest of honor was not asked to give a speech. Instead, he was interviewed by a panel of fellow writers, and this experiment worked so well that the American Center continued it the following season. In October, Robert Penn Warren was questioned by Harvey Breit and Elizabeth Janeway; in November, Norman Mailer by Charles Rolo and William Styron; in December, W. H. Auden by Daniel Hoffman and Louis Simpson; and in the following February John O'Hara answered the questions of two book reviewers. This format was still used occasionally in the following decade, and there was an especially glorious evening in January of 1962. Marianne Moore had agreed to be questioned by Louise Bogan, and then, since she was clearly enjoying herself, she took wing independently and alternately teased and instructed her delighted audience.

Out-of-town members who could not come to these meetings were obviously missing a great deal, and a solution was found in the expansion of the newsletter. Up to now there had been only a brief annual report sent out to the membership, its contents so restricted that the final issue, that of June 1952, used only seven lines to describe the nine dinners that had been held that season. When the newsletter was revised in November of 1954 it became a monthly with a greatly expanded format, and one member sent in a letter of approval immediately: "I like the *P.E.N. News.* For people like me who can never come to meetings it gives one a sense of still belonging to the Club."

The dinner meetings were fully reported in the *News,* recounting what had been said in what were sometimes highly readable little essays. Not only did they record "things too good to be forgotten," but they usually managed to be remarkably accurate. As Mailer said gratefully, it was wonderful not to be misquoted.

The monthly dinners had the further advantage of supplementing the cocktail parties as a way of entertaining foreign visitors. A P.E.N. member from Brussels attended a dinner at which Katherine Anne Porter and Glenway Wescott were among the speakers and she and her husband enjoyed themselves very much. They especially enjoyed "the friendly atmosphere we found. . . . Friendship is a thing as old as the world."

Part of this sense of warmth and friendliness was the gift of
the Secretary of the P.E.N.—Arthur James Putnam, whom everyone called Jim. A well-known editor, he had been elected to
the post of Secretary in the spring of 1952, and a short time
later he assumed the post of paid secretary also. In this latter
office Putnam had his difficulties, since there was never quite
enough money to supply him with the regular services of a
typist and his experience as an editor did not prepare him for
the minutiae of his position. (One member, who was delinquent
in her dues, finally paid up with the remark, "It was your
struggle over spelling 'deductible' that finally won me over.")
Whatever his lack of business training, Putnam more than made
up for it by his grace of mind, his loving nature, and his ardent
concern for the welfare of all writers. Insofar as the American
Center had a headquarters it was his apartment, and in it he
carried on the continuity of kindness that Bessie Beatty had
begun, supplying to a degree the place of "fellowship" of
which she had dreamed. As one member said gratefully in the
spring of 1957, "Every large family should have a James
Putnam."

Back in January of 1952, when a panel of editors discussed
"What's Wrong with Writers" at a P.E.N. dinner, Putnam was the
moderator. He was so successful that he moderated most of the
panels that winter, and his interest in the problems of writers
made him ideal for the job. In the autumn of 1956, he organized and moderated a series of eight panels sponsored jointly
by the American Center, and the Columbia Institute of Arts
and Sciences. The series was entitled, "How and Why Authors
Write," and the audience got its money's worth. One evening,
for instance, was on the theatre and the speakers were Robert
Anderson, Marc Connelly and Elmer Rice; another was on
poetry, with Louise Bogan, Langston Hughes and Phyllis McGinley. In 1958 a second series of this kind was presented and
the co-sponsor was New York University at Washington Square.
The first three years of this new series were moderated by
Putnam and the final year by Harding Lemay.

Since his French was fluent and his circle of friends very
large, James Putnam was a frequent delegate to the P.E.N. Con-

gresses. He went with James Farrell to Nice in 1952, with Henry Steele Commager to Dublin in 1953, and was the delegate whose plane fare to Amsterdam was paid by the Farfield Foundation in 1954.

The following year, the Farfield Foundation paid over a thousand dollars for the transportation of two delegates to the Congress in Vienna, and one of them made an ardent appeal for a much larger representation from the American Center. This delegate also felt, very strongly, that one of the International Vice-Presidents of the P.E.N. ought to be an American.

In 1956, the International Congress was held in London, and the Farfield Foundation paid the fare of Elmer Rice, as official delegate, from New York and that of Ralph Ellison, as one of the Congress guests of honor, from Rome. Ellison was deeply impressed by the Congress, a "tremendous job . . . carried out by David Carver, Veronica Wedgwood, John Lehmann and the countless lords and ladies and just plain writers." David Carver had succeeded his good friend, Hermon Ould, in the office of International Secretary and was carrying on the same tradition of capable and dedicated service. Ellison added, "Having seen the International Congress in action, I have a much more profound respect for the New York P.E.N. and its possibilities."

The American P.E.N. had a special share in the festivities in London, for it was host to all the delegates at a gala lunch on the eleventh of July. The lunch was given at the Guildhall, the oldest of the City Halls as well as "the most historic and splendid." It was in the Guildhall that General Eisenhower had received the sword of the City of London, and it supplied an impressive background for a very successful gathering. The American Ambassador was present, and in his brief address he justly praised the P.E.N. for "thinking in terms of all that draws men together as opposed to what sets them apart." As C. V. Wedgwood, the President of the English Center, said afterwards, "It was a deeply happy and truly memorable occasion."

It had not been easy to raise the money to pay for the lunch. The American Center had sent an appeal to its membership for contributions, but the money was very slow in coming in. Then

it suddenly became clear that the original sum would be much
too low, since another two hundred and fifty delegates had
signed up for the Congress. (The London *Times* called it "the
largest international meeting of authors ever assembled.") The
American Center made an emergency appeal to its members in
June, and this time the contributions poured in. For the appeal
not only pointed out the vital importance of being good hosts
in London but it carried the welcome news that the American
Center had at last achieved tax exemption.

The Center had been struggling for this over a long period of
time. A decade earlier, tax exemption had been granted for a
single, limited purpose—that of sending relief packages to Europe
—but in those days the Center was not doing anything of an
educational or cultural nature that would entitle it to special
consideration from Washington. In recent years, however, the
situation had been changing. The vigorous activities which had
started in 1951 had become firmly established, and the American Center was moving, sturdily and consistently, along the
lines of which Galsworthy had dreamed.

The responsibility for getting tax exemption in time for the
London Congress had been assumed by a single member of the
American Center—the distinguished New York jurist, Julius
Isaacs. The previous year he had revised the bylaws to bring
them up to date, and he brought the same vigorous sense of
order to his new task. In his presentation to the Treasury
Department, he stressed the long history of International P.E.N.,
the value of the literary and educational work that the American
Center was now able to do, and the responsibility it was assuming
in its relationship to writers all over the world. The State Department had indicated more than once its sense of the increasing
value of the Center, and Judge Isaacs was sure that the Treasury
Department would agree. Nevertheless, the speed with which
the Department moved was almost incredible. The application
was filed on the 23rd of May, 1956, and it was granted on the
6th of June, only ten working days later.

The importance of this tax exemption became very clear the
following year. In September of 1957, the International Congress was held in Tokyo, the first time there had ever been one

in Asia. The Japanese took the event very seriously (even department stores and school children were making donations) and, in spite of the heavy expenses in connection with transportation, the American Center wanted to make its delegation as large and as representative as possible.

Thanks to its new status as a tax-exempt organization, the American Center was given over ten thousand dollars by the Asia Foundation to send over a group of writers which included John Dos Passos, John Hersey and Elizabeth Janeway. It also included Elizabeth Gray Vining, whom the Japanese P.E.N. wanted as a guest of honor because she had been the tutor of the Crown Prince.

The Farfield Foundation had already made a grant of over five thousand dollars to pay for the transportation of the two official delegates from the American Center as well as that of a second guest of honor. The two delegates were Elmer Rice, who had a worldwide reputation as a playwright, and Donald Keene, one of the most distinguished translators from the Japanese. The guest of honor was John Steinbeck, who was deeply loved in Japan and whose writings were taught respectfully in its schools.

John Steinbeck had been approached on the subject the previous February by the President of the American Center, and he was more alarmed than pleased. He was attracted by the idea of the Tokyo Congress, for he had grown up with the Japanese in California and he also knew how much they loved his work, but he did not want to reverse the policy of a lifetime.

> I have always avoided meetings and congresses and clubs. And as far as I know I have never made a speech in my life. The very idea scares me to death. . . . I am also worried that one acceptance would let down the bars. . . . It becomes increasingly difficult for a writer to find time to write. It is considered that he should do everything else first. . . . The only answer is to turn mean for the sake of getting my own work done.

"And yet," Steinbeck added, "I do not feel mean." Moreover, he was greatly drawn to the idea of visiting Japan. "I have refused and probably will continue to refuse, but give me a little argument, will you?" The argument that was given was the obvious one—a reiteration of what P.E.N. stood for—and John Steinbeck went to Tokyo.

His speech at the opening ceremonies was one of the briefest on record, but it "deeply impressed" the delegates.

> I have a close relation with this congress. It's the first P.E.N. Congress held in Asia. It is my first congress anywhere.
>
> When I left New York I was very apprehensive about what to expect. A close friend said: "You will be all right. Just listen."
>
> But I found that listening is not enough. One should also hear. There are many reasons for listening. Some good and some devious. But the only purpose of hearing is understanding. I go now to listen and I hope to hear.

Almost at once, Steinbeck became ill and could take no part in the Congress, and when he returned to the United States he wrote a letter of apology to James Putnam. "No one can be happy with my performance in Tokyo. After the first two days except for Dos Passos and Hersey I never saw anyone—except Japanese. They were in my room eighteen hours a day." He characteristically did not mention that one of these visitors to his room was a Japanese girl who had read his work in translation and who had walked fifty miles to Tokyo hoping to have a glimpse of him. The hotel turned her away, and for two nights she slept in doorways. Then she tried again and tore her kimono on the barbed wire that blocked the entrance. Finally a houseboy told Steinbeck. Steinbeck not only invited her in, but he got up and dressed, with a fever of 104 degrees, so that he could escort her back through the lobby of the hotel.

The Tokyo Congress was a very successful one, and Donald Keene was able to report that serious attention was given to the subject of translation. "Perhaps no people reads as much literature in translation as the Japanese. . . . The most important work of the Congress was probably the resolution adopted on the subject." It urged that P.E.N. "should do all in its power to raise the general status of translators," and made five specific recommendations which included the awarding of prizes and the special training of translators.

There was very little argument on this resolution, since all the delegates, in theory at least, were in cordial agreement on the subject. Where the Tokyo Congress erupted in bitter debate was in connection with a resolution on the subject of the Hungarian Center of P.E.N.

The rising of the Hungarian people against the domination of the Communists had taken place eleven months earlier, in October of 1956, and the writers of Hungary had been in the forefront of the battle. One of those who managed to escape said that it had been "very encouraging and gratifying to see the signature of the P.E.N. Club on many placards, placed around the many places where fighting was going on." When the uprising failed, the Austrian P.E.N. Center in Vienna found itself struggling to help wave after wave of refugees; the American Center sent twelve hundred dollars to Vienna to assist the Secretary there as much as it could in her valiant effort to find food and shelter for the Hungarians.

Some of these Hungarian writers managed to get to the United States, and work was found for them throughout the country by various sponsoring organizations. The American Center sent a letter to each refugee, "telling of our concern for them as writers and asking what their needs are. Nearly all of them have jobs, although usually of a menial sort, but we shall have enough money to supply them with a Hungarian-English dictionary and also typewriter rental for a month or two, which in many cases should do more for their morale than anything else." The money came from a small grant by the Farfield Foundation. The dictionary was the best that could be obtained, the one put out by the Hungarian Academy of Sciences, and the keys of the typewriters were altered to conform to Hungarian usage.

Among those who received one of these typewriters was a very successful Hungarian novelist, Claire Kenneth. In an earlier struggle against tyranny she had resisted the Nazi regime, and Eisenhower gave her special honor after World War II for saving the lives of so many American pilots. Later, when it was the Communists who became the oppressors, Claire Kenneth resisted them also. "I fled Hungary in January 1957, after the revolution. I spent the last years in a forced labor camp. . . .

My husband, a nobleman, worked in a coal mine." After she
arrived in America, she "met Mr. Putnam, the secretary of the
P.E.N. Club. He was a very charming, wonderful gentleman."
When Claire Kenneth received her typewriter she started writing
again, and her new novels, translated into English, now reached
an American audience also.

There were many other Hungarians who had heroically resisted the dictatorship of both the Nazis and the Communists,
and the most famous of these was the novelist, Tibor Dery.
Along with Julius Hay and twenty-three others, he was arrested
in April of 1957 on a charge of complicity in the revolt, and
after a secret trial he was sentenced to nine years in prison. The
Hungarian Center of the P.E.N. made no protest, and it seemed
to some of the other Centers that it was becoming an apologist
for a totalitarian regime.

This was the situation that faced the P.E.N. delegates when
they gathered in September of that year in Tokyo. On the Congress agenda was a resolution presented by the Center for Writers
in Exile, which stated that the Hungarian Center had violated
the Charter by its tacit support of the current regime and should
be suspended. The President of the Hungarian Center, for his
part, had written a three-page justification of its position.

There were two points of view among the delegates, and both
were supported with complete sincerity and great energy. The
first was that the Club faced a time of testing similar to that at
the Dubrovnik Congress, that "great day . . . when P.E.N. stood
firm to its values and its ideals." The second was that P.E.N.
now faced a different problem altogether.

Galsworthy had dreamed of an organization which, in Forster's
words, was to be immune to "the accidents of government, language, race and color." Again and again, the links that P.E.N.
had tried to forge between the writers of the world had been
broken by war or revolution or conquest, but the dream remained. It had been very well expressed by a Hungarian writer
who had outlived the Nazi dictatorship and who, in 1946, had
received a gift package from the American Center. "We Hungarian writers who survived these years . . . feel now the importance
of being members of the P.E.N., standing behind us as a home of
the spirit."

Both points of view were valid, and the problem was debated with some bitterness at the Tokyo Congress. It was finally decided to suspend the Hungarian Center for the time being while a Committee of Five made a thorough investigation of the charges against it. This Committee of Five was made up of members of international standing, and the following June it had reached agreement. "The Hungarian Centre has made what appears to be a reasonable effort, within the context of the political climate in Budapest, to put its house to some extent in order. . . . That being so it would appear . . . to be the best course to accept their claim, lift the suspension . . . and watch very carefully what transpires."

Whether the various Centers would be willing to accept the recommendation of the Committee of Five was another matter, and in the American Center the Board had what was "a very long and, at times, heated discussion of the subject." The Board had been thoroughly briefed, and the discussion was intelligent and well informed. In the end, neither side could get a majority, and the final instruction to the American delegates to the 1959 Congress at Frankfurt was to abstain in the vote on the Hungarian question.

Meanwhile there was no abstaining from the struggle to get Tibor Dery and Julius Hay out of prison. The International P.E.N. and several individual Centers kept up a containing pressure, and in 1959 the American Center issued its own "call to conscience," an open letter to the Hungarian government with 259 signatures.*

> We, the undersigned American writers, wish to call
> attention to the fact that the Hungarian government still holds
> in prison many of the leading Hungarian writers and intellec-
> tuals, including the noted authors, Tibor Dery and Julius Hay.

*Arranging for an appeal of this kind had its difficulties, since the American Center had no office space, no staff and no real organization. When a special mailing had to be made, the usual procedure was for volunteers to stuff the envelopes at home in that honorable P.E.N. tradition that goes back to Galsworthy. One one occasion, when the envelopes had been stamped and sealed and were ready for mailing, it was discovered that a vital enclosure had been accidentally omitted. In this case, the home background of the operation turned out to be very useful; the volunteers who had been working on the mailing resorted to a steam iron and managed to steam all the envelopes open again.

> These men have been imprisoned for alleged crimes against
> the State, without public trials and without proper judicial
> procedure.
>
>   We therefore join with Albert Camus, T. S. Eliot, Karl
> Jaspers, Erich Kastner, François Mauriac, Alberto Moravia
> and Ignazio Silone in appealing to the conscience of the
> Hungarian government, as a member of the community of
> nations, either to give these men fair public trials immediately
> or to release them from prison.

This was forwarded in December of 1959 to the United
States delegate at the United Nations, and it received very wide
publicity overseas. There was no answer, however, from Hungary. In fact, the Hungarian government made it clear that the
P.E.N. would do well not to press for the release of the imprisoned writers, and the optimists who had voted for the continued
existence of the Hungarian Center began to wonder if they had
made a mistake.

They had not. The P.E.N. International Executive Committee
was scheduled to meet on the 4th of April, 1960, and a few days
earlier the glorious news arrived that Dery and Hay had been released. There was no question of any further proceedings
against the Hungarian Center, and its new President was able to
attend that year's P.E.N. Congress in Rio de Janeiro. Three years
later, when the International Executive Committee met at
Brighton, it was "the first time for some years that the Hungarian delegation did not have to report on writers in prison in
Budapest, since the April amnesty had freed the last of them—
including Istvan Bibo on whose behalf the P.E.N. had made
many representations in the recent past. . . . The President of
the Hungarian Centre . . . invited the International Executive
to hold the second 1964 half-yearly meeting at Budapest . . .
and his invitation was greeted with warm applause and unanimously accepted." The links between the Centers had held,
and the optimists had been justified.

The Congress of 1960 which met in Rio de Janeiro set up a
permanent Writers in Prison Committee. It also passed a manifesto urging that released writers should be permitted to work
again, as part of a general effort "to re-establish the freedom of

writing wherever it is suppressed." It was fitting that the delegate from the American Center to this Congress in South America was Elmer Rice, for he cared deeply about this particular
subject.

When Rice joined the P.E.N. back in 1939, he had not expected to be particularly useful. "The Authors League and the
American Civil Liberties Union take a great deal of my time,
and trying to be an author, director and producer seems to
occupy what is left." Nevertheless, he found in the P.E.N. an
echo of his own ardent concern for mental freedom, and in
fact he became so invaluable that in 1958 he was "elected unanimously and with much acclaim . . . to be a Vice-President of
the International P.E.N." This was the first time in the history
of P.E.N. that an American had been made an International
Vice-President, and it was a mark of how far the American Center had come in its determination to take its international obligations seriously.

Thanks to the continuing financial support of the Farfield
Foundation, it was now possible for the American Center to
send delegates regularly not only to the Congresses but to the
meetings of the International Executive Committee. It was
also possible for the Center to be represented at other meetings
of international importance, such as the translators' conference
that was held at Warsaw in 1958.

Up to now the American Center had not shown any special
zeal on the subject of translation, in spite of the vigorous effort
that had been made by Henry Seidel Canby in the late 1920's.
When the P.E.N. Charter was approved in its final form in 1948,
it carried the statement that membership was open "to all qualified writers, editors and translators," but in this same year Jane
Hudson was obliged to report, "No translators are members of
the American Center of P.E.N."

In 1951, Wallace Stegner suggested the possibility of estab-
lishing "a committee on translation of books from other countries, particularly Asian." The following spring, a committee
was set up "to investigate the need for and financing of translations," but the chairman went abroad to live and the committee
went out of existence.

By this time, the long negotiations that International P.E.N. had been conducting with UNESCO on the subject of translation were beginning to show results, and the responsibility of individual Centers was correspondingly lessened. Some of the Centers, however, took individual action. The Japanese Center set up a Translation Committee of its own in 1954, and when the P.E.N. Congress met in Tokyo three years later there were long discussions on the subject. The result was the final resolution on translation that was passed by the Congress, and Donald Keene, who had helped to bring it into being, carried a copy of it around with him until it became dog-eared.

The Polish Center had "always given special attention to the problem," and in 1958 it was one of the sponsors of a three-day conference on translation in Warsaw. It was "a pioneer gathering of disinterested workers in a difficult field," conducted mostly in French, and the American Center was able to send delegates.

One of these delegates was the editor and publisher, Theodore Purdy. He was very much impressed by the Warsaw conference and promised his colleagues in Poland that the American Center would investigate the possibility of an "organized program" on translation. The incoming President in the spring of 1959 was so impressed by Purdy's report that she set up a Translation Committee. This was a direct result of the Warsaw conference, and a very durable one.

Purdy served as chairman for the first four years, and both writers and editors were included. This meant that practical problems could be argued face to face and practical solutions reached. The Committee did not concern itself with technical and scientific translation, since this was not within the scope of the P.E.N. Its concern was with literary translation—the transference of the voice of the creator into an alien tongue—and its purpose was to give the translator at least some measure of the dignity and security that his function deserved. For, as the President of the Polish Center had pointed out during the Warsaw conference, the translator "is moved by the same exaltations as the writer, when he is animated by the certainty that he works at something imperishable."

The vigor of the Translation Committee was only one example of the kind of energy that the American Center was able to show now that it had regained a sense of purpose, and the changes that had taken place in a single decade can be measured by comparing the annual business meeting that took place in May of 1950 with the same one in May ten years later. In the first instance, there had been a poorly attended luncheon at the New Weston Hotel, and there was almost nothing for the Secretary to report in the way of activities except four dinners, one cocktail party and the "admirable job" done by the Admissions Committee. Now, in May of 1960, the dinner was a gala affair, very well attended, and it took a long time for the Secretary to report all the activities of the past year.

The emphasis was on internationalism, and one very pleasant aspect of it was the reception which the American Center had given the previous September for the International Institute of Ibero-American Literature which was meeting in New York. The affair was a great success. "In spite of the pouring rain, eighty P.E.N. members turned up to welcome about the same number of guests, and the Spanish-speaking members like Langston Hughes . . . were in constant demand as each group struggled cheerfully with the language and usually managed to surmount it."

The reception had been held, very appropriately, in the Carnegie Endowment International Center Building. The building was dedicated to the cause of good will among nations, and it had a large room whose high windows looked out on the trees of the United Nations Plaza. It was in this same room that the American Center held its May dinner the following spring, to hear the officers' reports, to conduct elections and to enjoy each other's company.

The guest of honor at this May dinner in 1960 was Yasunari Kawabata, President of the Japanese Center and an International Vice President of P.E.N. (Eight years later, he became the first Japanese writer to be given the Nobel Prize.) He was still looking like a "small and thoughtful lion," as one of the delegates to the Tokyo Congress had described him, and in his brief speech at the May dinner he expressed his pleasure at the distinction of the delegation that the American Center had sent to Tokyo.

It was at this Tokyo Congress that the question of translation had received special attention, and now, three years later, the Secretary of the American Center was able to announce, as one of the accomplishments of the past season, the establishment of the Translation Committee under the chairmanship of Theodore Purdy. Another achievement was the wide publicity that had been given the open letter to the Hungarian government on behalf of Tibor Dery and Julius Hay. "It was broadcast by Radio Free Europe to a number of Middle European countries, with a list of prominent signers and in some cases with special interviews." P.E.N. had contributed its full share to the pressure for the release of the two men—a release which had taken place less than two months before this dinner in May.

The President of the previous year was re-elected to a second term and in a speech of acceptance reiterated the commitment that had become so clear in the course of the past decade. "I will continue to do everything I can to further the work of P.E.N. and to strengthen this international link of good will and creative energy, this sense that writers have an enduring responsibility to join together in the cause of good understanding and mutual respect between nations, since, in the words of our P.E.N. Charter, 'literature . . . knows no frontiers.' "

The main speaker of the evening was Harrison Salisbury, an expert in Russian affairs, and during his speech he emphasized the glorious record of some of the writers there. "We in the West have underestimated the power of writers to withstand suppression. The spark of free human spirit in the Russian writers makes them our allies in spite of political barriers." It was this alliance of the spirit that the P.E.N. had been created to encourage, and at long last the American Center had begun to play its part in helping to make it a continuing reality.

Part Four

When the International Executive Committee of the P.E.N. met in Rome in 1961, the American delegation was asked if its Center would be host to a Congress in 1964. America was a very rich country, and the Center could surely afford it.

It was explained to the Executive Committee that the country was rich, but the American Center was not. The question of possible support had been talked over with foundations, but no "positive commitment" of any kind had been achieved. As for the American government, it had traditionally shown no interest in the arts, and it had no sense of obligation toward the success of a P.E.N. Congress. This was a difficult thing for Europeans to understand, since their own governments supported these Congresses and valued them.*

Elmer Rice had been an International Vice-President for three years now, and he was very well aware of the nature of this mis-

* The universities of Europe felt the same. When the P.E.N. Congress was held in Amsterdam in 1954, the University of Leyden conferred honorary degress on three of the delegates. They moved to the Senate House at the head of a procession which consisted of all the faculty and the rest of the Congress delegates, who were then received by the Lord Mayor. Everything was in perfect, ceremonial order, including the fact that each of the three Doctors was presented at dinner, according to custom, with "an enormous cake decorated with an allegorical scene in marzipan."

understanding. Two years later, in June of 1963, he told the
Board of the American Center that it was "very difficult" for
the writers of other countries to understand why the writers of
the United States had not offered to hold a P.E.N. Congress.

It could at least be said that the American Center was able to
entertain individual writers from abroad. In this particular
year of 1963, for instance, the afternoon receptions at the
Pierre included a great many foreigners. In January there were
three guests from Russia, in February two from India, in March
a Welsh novelist and a member of the Board of the Argentine
P.E.N., in April a publisher from Stockholm and a poet from the
Jamaica Center. Later in this same April there was a reception
for a single guest of honor—Ignazio Silone of Italy, the distinguished novelist who was also an International Vice-President of
P.E.N.

The dinner meetings in 1963 were all held at the Overseas
Press Club and were very well planned. The February dinner
was a panel on "The Problems of the Negro Writer" and the
speakers were Ralph Ellison, Langston Hughes and LeRoi Jones.*
The March dinner had a single speaker—August Heckscher, whom
President Kennedy had just appointed to the newly created post
of Special Consultant on the Arts. Kennedy had declined membership in the P.E.N. when he was a Senator but he joined the
organization after he became President, and it was clear that
the government of the United States had become willing to take
writers seriously. The fact that Robert Frost took part in the
Inauguration was a symbol of this, and Frost was scheduled to
be the speaker at the P.E.N. dinner in April. When the news
came of his death, the evening was changed into a memorial to
him. President Kennedy sent a message that he joined with his
"fellow members of P.E.N. in paying tribute to a great artist
and American."

The following month, in May of 1963, came the annual dinner
for the transaction of business and the election of officers. The occasion was a milestone for the Translation Committee: Harry Scherman of the Book-of-the-Month Club was presenting an award of a

---

* LeRoi Jones has since changed his name to Imamu Amiri Baraka.

thousand dollars for the best translation into English of a foreign-language work of literature published during the year in the United States. One of the three judges was Lewis Galantière, and he gave the address on that memorable evening, describing what the American Center had already achieved in the field of translation and what it hoped to achieve in the future.

In December of the same year there was another milestone for the American Center: the Farfield Foundation gave two thousand dollars toward the expenses of holding an International Congress in New York. The Foundation was much too small to consider defraying the whole of the cost, but the two thousand dollars served as seed money so that other foundations could be approached in earnest.

The Congress of the United States was not willing to vote any money for international cultural programs, no matter how admirable they might be. On the other hand, it was willing to vote huge sums to the Central Intelligence Agency without demanding an accounting, and as a result a kind of *opéra bouffe* situation had developed in recent years. The C.I.A. passed some of the money on to various small foundations of impeccable reputation, and these in turn passed it on to "student, religious, union, cultural and other groups" in support of a variety of international programs. What was thus created, in the words of *The New York Times,* was "an intricate web of interlocking foundations and other sources of funds . . . involving many private organizations whose officers had not been aware that some of their support was coming from the C.I.A."

It was not until 1967 that this secret funding was discovered. There was an immediate uproar, since a clandestine operation of this kind, and under such auspices, was clearly intolerable. On the other hand, it was also clear that some fifteen million dollars a year had been spent in support of programs that were greatly needed and that such "C.I.A. orphans" as school bands traveling in Europe could hardly be left stranded. A government committee was set up to devise some kind of alternate funding, but it was finally obliged to report that it had "failed to reach agreement on means of open public financing."

The Farfield Foundation was one of the many that were involved in this "web of interlocking foundations." It had been
getting some of its money from another foundation which in
turn was supported by the C.I.A. As soon as this was discovered,
the Board of the American Center voted to end the relationship
with the Farfield Foundation and sent out this decision to the
membership, making it clear at the same time how wholly it
disapproved of "the use of secret funds."

Back in 1963 there was, of course, no hint of all this subsequent history, and the grant of two thousand dollars of seed
money from the Farfield Foundation was received with gratitude. Work on the Congress was begun immediately, and in
June it was possible to extend an invitation for a Congress to be
held in New York in 1966.

When the last P.E.N. Congress had been held in New York,
back in 1924, there had been only eighteen Centers. Now they
existed all over the world, and the P.E.N. Congresses were
events of international interest. More than that, they had
become a kind of symbol of P.E.N.'s durability in a bitterly
divided and tormented world.

The Congress of 1965, the one immediately preceding the
gathering in New York, was in Yugoslavia, at Bled. The last
time a Congress had been held in Yugoslavia was in 1933, when
the P.E.N. delegates at Dubrovnik had resisted the first creeping
Nazi threat to their freedom. After the War was over, it took a
long time for the Center in Yugoslavia to come back into existence,
but it was finally re-established in 1962 with several branches.

Some of the P.E.N. Centers threatened to boycott the Bled
Congress of 1965 because the Yugoslav writer, Mihajlo Mihajlov,
had been imprisoned by the government. The optimists in P.E.N.
were opposed to this boycott, especially since the Slovene
branch, which was the host of this 1965 Congress, had joined
in the protests against the imprisonment. Again the optimists
were justified; a month before the Bled Congress was due to
open, Mihajlov was given a suspended sentence.

Back in 1944, when the bombs were falling on London,
E. M. Forster attended the conference on *Areopagitica* with his
faith in P.E.N. undiminished. "Why . . . do we meet? . . . For two

reasons. We want to clear up our own ideas about the future if we can because it is a pleasure and a duty to get the mind clear; and secondly, though we cannot hope to cut any ice we may succeed in melting a little." The future had come with its fears and its repressions, with the glaring suspicions of the cold war and the growth of an almost unchecked nationalism. Yet the P.E.N. never forgot why it had come into existence, and, patiently and hopefully, it continued on the course it had set for itself.

The Bled Congress would have delighted Galsworthy, for even the Russians came. It is true that they came only as observers, since no one had yet found a way to adjust the current Russian policy to the principles of the P.E.N. Charter. It is also true that they were somewhat stiff and formal at first, but they grew progressively more friendly.

In a further effort to relax the atmosphere at Bled, the usual policy of a set of formal speeches was changed to a series of Round Tables, so that the discussion among the participants could be direct and relatively informal. The experiment had its disadvantages. Space was limited, so that only a few P.E.N. members could be admitted to the Round Tables. Moreover, there was no way of recording the discussions, which survived each day only in the notes that were taken by the various chairmen. These were passed on to the membership, however, by a "remarkably alert, fluent and witty rapporteur," and the advantage of writers talking to one another instead of listening to set papers was considerable. It extended the art of corridor conversation, which was the great strength of most Congresses, and officially recognized its existence.

Another unique aspect of the Bled Congress was its choice of a new International President. For the first time in the history of P.E.N., he was an American—the playwright Arthur Miller. Like P.E.N., Miller was respected on both sides of the Iron Curtain, and it was a sign of how unanimously he was approved that his nomination was made by the Yugoslavs themselves. He made a superb International President—eloquent, hardworking and deeply concerned with that liberty of the spirit that so concerned the P.E.N. itself.

The President of the American Center was Lewis Galantière, who had accepted the office with full awareness that he would be responsible for the success of next year's Congress in New York. He went to Bled as an official delegate, and the other delegate was Julius Isaacs, who had been working ardently for several years on the project. In fact, as Galantière said later, it was Isaacs "to whose initiative and insistence the Congress owed its existence."

As for Galantière himself, he determined to make the New York Congress of 1966 a continuation of all that had been most hopeful and imaginative at Bled, and he dropped for a time his work with every other organization so that he could achieve this extremely difficult aim.

He was confronted with one situation in connection with the forthcoming Congress which was watched with a good deal of curiosity abroad. The Slovene Center had been confronted with a potentially embarrassing problem when the Yugoslav government refused to release Mihajlov, but the American Center faced the possibility of a much greater embarrassment. Fot it was the policy of the government of the United States not to issue visas to writers who were suspected of being troublemakers, Communists, or otherwise unsuitable for entry.

Back in 1957, just before John Steinbeck went to the Tokyo Congress, he asked some of his friends in the P.E.N. why no Congress was being planned in the United States; he was told that it would be impossible to obtain visas for many of the delegates. Steinbeck then amused himself by drawing up a list of the great men of history who would have been refused entry, from King David ("revolution") to Socrates ("contributing to moral delinquency of minors"). As Steinbeck pointed out, even the signers of the Declaration of Independence would not be welcome, since they would have to admit to rebellion and treason.

This was the major problem that faced the New York Congress, surpassing even the difficult one of financing it. It would be useless to call the occasion an International Congress if the delegates from the Cuban Center were to be refused entry. Yet Cuba was a Communist country and a deeply mistrusted enemy ever since the missile crisis in the administration of the late President Kennedy.

It is one of the basic principles of the P.E.N. that writers should never be judged by the activities of their governments, and Galantière started very early and very carefully to prepare the ground with the State Department. In June of 1965, he was officially informed that the Department would not object to the participation of a Cuban delegation in the New York Congress, and an invitation went out in the regular way to the Cuban Center. A second invitation went out the same day to its President. No answer came back in either case, but it was not the fault of the American Center that the Cuban Center had not been able to avail itself of a similar freedom.

The Russians promised to send observers, as they had at Bled. The observers' names were listed in the program of the Congress, but, at the last moment, they received countermanding orders and were not able to appear. Nor did three of the delegates from Czechoslovakia put in an appearance; their passports had been suddenly recalled. On the other hand, the East German delegation arrived in full strength, a little morose and suspicious in the beginning but gradually thawing into real cordiality.

At the Congress itself, the American Center sponsored a resolution which was passed unanimously. It put the P.E.N. on record as disapproving of "measures taken by any government which have the effect of preventing P.E.N. members from leaving their own country or entering a foreign country" in order to attend a P.E.N. meeting. The free movement of writers could sometimes be as important as the free movement of books, and every victory of this kind set a precedent for the next one.

The honestly international tone of the New York Congress was greatly assisted by the fact that Arthur Miller was the International President. When his name came up for re-election, there was no discussion. "What is there to discuss? We can only vote him our profound thanks." Miller understood very well what the P.E.N. was about, and when he made the opening address to the New York Congress on the 13th of June, he emphasized a point that could not be made too often. "None of us comes here as a representative of his country. None of us is

obliged to speak here as an apologist for his culture or his political system." Instead, it was the privilege of the P.E.N. to offer
all writers "a neutral ground, a kind of sanctuary," where they
could rest on a reality which had nothing to do with any political divisions—"the stubborn, underlying sameness of the human
spirit whatever the variety of forms in which it is expressed."

Galantière had this same clear sense of the things of the spirit
and the value of P.E.N. as neutral ground, and he made a special
and vigorous effort to see that Africa, Asia and Latin America
were adequately represented at the New York Congress by
writers of distinction. In fact, he made it possible for eleven
countries which still possessed no P.E.N. Centers to send observers to New York. In Africa, for instance, the Ivory Coast P.E.N.
Center and the one in Senegal sent delegates, but African writers
came also as observers from Ghana, Kenya and Nigeria. In Central and South America, the Centers in Argentina, Brazil, Chile
and Uruguay sent delegates, but observers came also from Mexico,
Peru and Venezuela. On the closing day of the Congress, Roger
Caillois spoke for UNESCO, of which P.E.N. is an affiliate. He
described himself as deeply impressed by the unremitting effort
that had resulted in so large a representation of writers from all
over the world, and he felt that this had contributed in very large
part to the "magnificent success of the Congress."

Underneath this triumph—and it was a triumph—was the hard
fact that it cost a great deal of money. When the American invitation was extended at Oslo in 1964, it was done on faith; there
were no funds for the purpose. On the first of April, 1965, a
letter went out to the membership to tell them that they would
be hosts to seventy-five P.E.N. Centers in New York in 1966.
"What that means is hardly conceivable to an American who has
not attended a P.E.N. Congress in a foreign country. Heads of
state welcome P.E.N.; governments make palaces available; Minis-
tries of Culture contribute performances of the state opera and
the national theatre, defray the costs of brilliant receptions and
arrange tours to places of historic interest. . . . We, in this country, do things differently. . . . This is the first P.E.N. Congress
to be held in the United States in 41 years, and we must be
worthy hosts to our fellow writers from Europe, Asia, Australia

and the Americas." Each member was asked to send as large a contribution as he could, and it was because the membership responded so promptly and enthusiastically that it was possible to turn to the foundations.

The raising of the money was uphill work at first, but little by little the obvious importance of what was being attempted evoked a corresponding enthusiasm. In the end, the long list of the supporters of the Congress included publishers, manufacturers, associations and foundations of all types and sizes. Even the United States government, at last beginning to concern itself with what had so long concerned P.E.N., made a generous donation through the National Council on the Arts. The single largest gift came from the Ford Foundation; it was an indication of the position which American P.E.N. had at last achieved that this foundation, approached so many times in the past and always in vain, should have made so large a donation and considered the money very well spent.

During the long months of preparation, office space was made available in the Institute of International Education, located just opposite the United Nations. During the Congress itself, the headquarters was the Loeb Student Center of New York University at Washington Square. Loeb Center was fully equipped with offices and conference rooms, lounges, restaurants and an auditorium, so that all the official business of the Congress could be conducted under a single roof. The various University residence halls in the neighborhood of Washington Square were used to house the delegates, and it was a point of pride with everyone to make them feel at home. This was a section of New York which had a great many literary associations; for New York University had employed many writers as teachers, from Thomas Wolfe to Saul Bellow, and the curving streets of nearby Greenwich Village had always been the welcomers of poets and playwrights and novelists.

In its turn, the P.E.N. Congress provided its own set of literary memories. No one who met the great poet from Chile, Pablo Neruda, walking under the green trees of Washington Square on his way to one of the meetings, would be likely to forget him. Neruda had been one of the glories of the Bled

Congress, the first P.E.N. Congress he had ever attended, but since he was a Communist very few people thought he would be willing to come to the United States or that the government would be willing to have him. Nevertheless, he was there, for P.E.N. had persuaded the State and Justice Departments to give him a visa without delay. Neruda was applauded and interviewed and followed about everywhere, and to the young people in particular his presence was one of the literary events of the year.

It took a great deal of planning to take advantage, in the New York Congress, of the Round Tables that had been used at Bled, and to continue their vigor and informality without importing any of their disadvantages. The halls in Loeb Center where the discussions were held were large enough to seat everyone who wanted to attend, and interpreters from the United Nations supplied the same professional services they gave the U.N. delegates. Some of the talk was brilliant, and none of it was lost, since all of it was put on tape and published in both English and French, in book form, as "Proceedings of the XXXIV International P.E.N. Congress."

The theme of the Congress was "The Writer as Independent Spirit," and the care with which it was chosen was characteristic of the whole Congress. Back in February of 1965, a ten-member committee was set up which consisted of Edward Albee, B. J. Chute, Leon Edel, Ralph Ellison, John Hersey, Elizabeth Janeway, Lenore Marshall, James Putnam, Elmer Rice and Glenway Wescott. They were looking for a theme which would "provide a springboard for important discussion and speeches; does not enter into the political area; does not repeat previous themes, and honors the writer as a creative being." Out of many hours of "very wide, far-ranging and prolonged" debate came the theme, which was unanimously approved by the Board. It contained such a variety of ways of approaching the central subject that the Round Tables had no shortage of topics for lively discussion.

The most remarkable of these Round Tables was an unscheduled one. The writers who gathered in New York from Central and South America admired each other's work but in most cases, because of the vast distances, they had never met each other in person. They had so much to talk about that Arthur Miller suggested they hold a Round Table of their own in the middle of the week, with the rest of the Congress listening in. It was a very stimulating meeting. Writers from Argentina, Brazil, Chile, Mexico, Peru, Uruguay and Venezuela talked earnestly, ardently and intently about the special problems that writers faced in these countries, and while they did not speak directly to the theme, their independence was clear in everything they said.

The Congress was not, of course, all discussion. A series of festivities had been planned for the pleasure of the delegates, and one of the most charming took place on June the twelfth, the Sunday of their arrival. It was called *pique-nique sur l'eau*, and the delegates were supplied with wine and music and picnic baskets while their boat circled the lower part of Manhattan and one of the most beautiful sunsets of the year lit up the Statue of Liberty. The party lasted four hours, and one of the French delegates delightedly termed it *"saisissant."* All New York was its background, and the rain which fell in the city that evening politely refrained from falling on the picnickers themselves. As *The New York Times* said, "No congress ever got off to a more engaging start."

The other special events of the Congress included receptions at the United Nations, at the American Academy and National Institute of Arts and Letters, and at the Museum of Modern Art. One evening, various members of the P.E.N. who lived in New York gave parties in their homes for the delegates, and at the end of the week there was a day in the country, with swimming and tennis, when hospitable residents of Long Island opened their houses to the guests from abroad.

The gala banquet which was the traditional climax of every P.E.N. Congress took place on Friday, the 17th of June, in the Grand Ballroom of the Plaza Hotel, which supplied the elegance and the candlelit grace that the evening required. In spite of its size this was a family party, and the Press, to its great astonishment, was not invited. Otherwise the magazines and newspapers were encouraged to pay close attention to the

Congress, which they did, and even at the *pique-nique sur l'eau*
interviews were given.

The Americans wanted very much to be good hosts, and there
were many volunteers to assist the small staff of professionals.
Since the Congress had been planned for a registration of 500
and the final total was 810, everything naturally ran short.
Emergencies occurred with such regularity that they became normal, and the harried individuals who manned the reception desk
sometimes felt that they were riding precariously on a wave that
was certain to break and engulf them. What they lacked, however, in calm order they made up for by their fervent desire that
everyone should feel at home. When the President of the American Center, in his brief address at the banquet, referred to
those "sweet-tempered, unruffled young women who served in
the front line of the melee," the audience broke into applause.

The following morning the Congress came to a close with a
series of speeches, and perhaps the most moving from the point
of view of these volunteers was the one given by Ignazio Silone,
veteran of many P.E.N. Congresses. He spoke of the style and
warmth of the New York Congress and said that he took away
one very striking impression: " Not one political figure, no minister of education, no mayor, no public authority spoke from
this platform." When the Americans issued the invitation they
had been acutely aware of how little they could expect from
officialdom, and it was a pleasure to know that what at the time
had seemed to be a handicap to the Congress had turned out in
the end to be one of its most distinctive and admirable features.

The following year, the Ivory Coast Center was host to the
P.E.N. Congress—the first time that one had been held in Africa.
Here also the welcome was very warm, but officialdom was once
more present. The opening ceremonies took place in the Con-
gressional Hall, with the President of the Republic and his Cabinet
Ministers in attendance, and the P.E.N. delegates ascended the
stairs between a double row of guards in scarlet and gold with
raised sabers.

Like all the others, this 1967 Congress at Abidjan took special note of the writers who were in prison in both Communist
and non-Communist countries; there were resolutions protesting

imprisonments in Czechoslovakia, Greece, Haiti, Portugal, Spain and South Vietnam. Above all, there was the case of the two Russian writers, Andrei Sinyavsky and Yuli Daniel, imprisoned in 1966 for what were termed "anti-Soviet slanders."

Such protests were usually presented by the International P.E.N., with the weight of all the Centers behind it, but in the case of the Russian writers the American Center asked for permission to take individual action. In January of 1967, it sent an appeal to the Russian government over the signatures of a long list of writers, editors and publishers—555 of them. It was a varied list, ranging from Allen Ginsberg to Hannah Arendt and from Thornton Wilder to P.G. Wodehouse, and many of the signers added a scrawled message to the Center—"Bravo, P.E.N." or "With all my heart."

The appeal was carefully worded, so that the request for amnesty would be a courteous one and not provocative; it even noted that "the long and liberal literary tradition of the Russian people would be confirmed by this gesture." Some P.E.N. members failed to notice that it was the Russian people and not their government that was being described and wrote in the margin, "This is nonsense!" or "Is P.E.N. kidding?" Nevertheless they signed, adding their voices to the rising chorus. One member wrote, "I do not believe that this protest will be effective in the Soviet Union but I think it is important to protest" as there was no other way to prevent injustices from being "steamrollered to oblivion." The Russian government gave no outward sign of being moved but both men were released before their prison terms had ended, Yuli Daniel in September of 1970 and Andrei Sinyavsky in June of 1971.

There was no need for the American Center to consult the International when the case involved an American writer. Late in this same year of 1967, for instance, LeRoi Jones was given a heavy sentence in New Jersey for the illegal possession of weapons; this was outside the province of P.E.N., but the judge made it clear that he had been influenced by a poem that the accused had written. The American Center gave immediate publicity to the case, vigorously protesting "the impropriety of any judge imposing a sentence, the severity of which is based on

his disapproval of the literary work of the accused." The case
went to the Court of Appeals, which did not make special note
of this point but which reversed the conviction on the ground
that the judge's whole charge to the jury had been improper and
prejudicial. Two years later, the Immigration Department
refused to permit the Mexican novelist, Carlos Fuentes, to land
on United States soil because his name was on a list of foreigners
who were considered "undesirable." The American Center
wired an immediate protest to the State Department, and when
Fuentes sent his "profound gratitude" to the Center he noted
that "once more P.E.N. has proved its immense value as an
active force in defense of the freedom of writers."

Carlos Fuentes already knew what might be expected of
P.E.N. He had been invited to come as an observer to the New
York Congress of 1966, and he had been both startled and impressed by what he called "the improbable spectacle of 500
writers—conservatives, anarchists, communists, liberals, social-
ists—meeting, not to underline their differences or to enunciate
their dogmas, but to . . . bear witness to the existence of a community of the spirit while accepting diversity of intentions."

This had been one of the great achievements of the New York
Congress. It was a visible manifestation of the pledge in the
Charter for "the unhampered transmission of thought within
each nation and between all nations," an open expression of
the conviction upon which the whole of P.E.N. rests.

Another achievement of the Congress was that it gave the
American Center an increased sense of energy, and an old
dream began to revive. It was the dream of having a central
headquarters, with a full-time secretary and enough money to
embark upon projects that even the most willing volunteers
could not undertake unaided. Interest in the P.E.N. was now
very high and a great many new members had joined, but the
obvious possibilities for growth were being choked off for lack
of room to operate.

The Congress itself had been lavishly supplied with office
space, but once it was over the American Center was obliged to
squeeze itself back into what was known as "Betsy Cenedella's
kitchen." Mrs. Cenedella had become the secretary of the P.E.N.

in 1965, working part time and in her own home as all the secretaries before her had done. She managed to fit the current
files into a corner of her kitchen and to keep up a complicated
correspondence with what was now a membership of nearly
nine hundred.

The back files of the P.E.N. were in the basement of James
Putnam's apartment building. He had resigned as secretary at
the beginning of the decade, but he amiably consented to store
the papers since there was nowhere else for them to go. When
he died the files had to be moved, and Daniel Melcher offered
to house them temporarily in the offices of *Publishers' Weekly,*
as his father before him had once done.

It was clear that the American Center had become intolerably
cramped just at the moment of its greatest possibility for growth,
and in January of 1967 a task force was set up. It consisted of
the President, Secretary and Treasurer (Lewis Galantière, Marshall Best and Julius Isaacs) and in March it was empowered by
the Board to submit "a plan for future operation of the Center
. . . to take advantage of the momentum generated by the New
York Congress." The task force, whose name was soon changed
to the Development Committee, drew up a careful, detailed
plan based on the acquisition of a downtown headquarters and
"a full-time paid Executive Secretary." This, in its turn, was of
course based on money, and an application for funds was made
to the National Council on the Arts.

Congress had been adjusting its priorities in recent years, and
by this time it was possible for an organization like the P.E.N.
to receive official support from the government. The National
Council on the Arts had been one of the major supporters of
the New York Congress, and it was equally pleased with the
plan for the future that was submitted to it by the Development
Committee in 1967. In November of that year, the Council
agreed to a grant of twenty thousand dollars if P.E.N. could
raise the matching funds.

P.E.N. could and did, and by the following spring the dream
had become a reality. On the 20th of May, 1968, the Board
paid a formal visit to the first permanent headquarters that the
American Center had ever had—two large rooms on the second

floor of an office building at Fifth Avenue and 20th Street. At
the same time, the Board had the pleasure of meeting Kirsten
Michalski, the full-time Executive Secretary. Mrs. Michalski had
formerly worked at the Institute of International Education,
and she was everything that the Club had hoped to find. A short
time later, Mrs. Cenedella resigned as Corresponding Secretary
so as to give more time to her lively small son, and her place was
taken by Barbara Rice. She was the widow of Elmer Rice, who
would have rejoiced in the coming-of-age of an organization on
which he had lavished so much time and affection. Between them,
the Executive Secretary and the Corresponding Secretary turned
the P.E.N. office into a place of welcome, and it was characteristic that when one of them lent her sangria jug for the center
table, the other filled it with leaves and flowers from the
country.

Neither the money from the government nor the matching
funds could be used to buy furniture and equipment, and the
problem of how to fill the empty rooms might have been a difficult one. When the English Center opened its headquarters in
London in 1927, Mrs. Dawson Scott supplied all the furnishings
with the exception of one ashtray, and five years later a special
request went out to ask someone to please donate a bookcase.
The American Center, on the other hand, did not have the
problem of getting equipment until it had been in existence
for nearly half a century and thus possessed a large and loyal
membership. Tables, chairs, handsome desks and even an
antique oak cabinet were given by the members, who also supplied smaller items ranging from a door buzzer and a pencil
sharpener to an electric plate and a whistling teakettle.

In January of 1969, the House Committee reported that
P.E.N. was still short of three items. "We need built-in bookshelves (P.E.N. without books?), folding chairs (for meetings
and discussion groups) and long and fairly heavy curtains for
the high windows which let in daylight but also let in drafts."
The Committee asked the members to send one dollar each,
and most of them were touched by the smallness of the sum.
One novelist wrote in to say that no organization, "not even
the Tenth Avenue Social and Athletic Club (to which I belonged
as a youth) asked for as little as a dollar," and he sent fifty.

Everything that the House Committee had mentioned was soon in existence. The gold curtains were hung in the large room where meetings were held; the folding chairs were stacked in a closet, ready to accommodate a large audience whenever the need arose. The second room was used as an office by the staff, and one of its walls, from floor to ceiling, was covered with the built-in bookshelves. Each member was asked to give the P.E.N. library a book of which he was especially proud, whether as an author, editor or translator, and by December of 1969 the shelves were gay with autographed copies. A Christmas party was held to celebrate this final addition to a completely furnished clubhouse. The walls were festooned with evergreen, and the current President, Charles Bracelen Flood, was so carried away by the general jubilation that he even thought briefly of dressing up as Santa Claus.

In the end he decided against it; yet it would have been a reasonable thing to do since he was one of those Presidents who have always turned up in the American Center when they were needed. In this case, what was required in the President was the ability to make use of the possibilities that were inherent in the new situation. The year before Flood was elected President, he had shown this kind of imaginative energy by inventing and heading a Grants and Awards Committee. It made a list of all the awards, fellowships, grants, and prizes available to writers, and by the end of the season it had issued two publications entitled "List of Grants and Awards"—one for the use of American writers and the other for the use of foreign writers coming to the United States.

This was the kind of project that the American Center could not have initiated until it had a headquarters of its own and a skilled and dedicated Executive Secretary. The lists have proved to be of such obvious value that every year since then they are brought up-to-date and reissued. A great many requests come from university libraries and from individual writers, and members of P.E.N. can order at half price.

Some of the innovations of the new administration did not require office space. There was, for instance, a new program called "P.E.N. in the City," with Sidney Offit as chairman. It was designed to make available "the services of P.E.N. members

to informal groups and institutions working with young people
in the ghetto," mostly through talks and workshops, and it
also has had a continuing existence. An organization which had
been set up to combat drug addiction called this P.E.N. program
"a huge contribution to human renewal" and said that it was
a "whole new world of achievement for our young people"
when some of their poetry was printed in the P.E.N. quarterly
in the spring of 1970.

This quarterly was another new venture and was named *The
American Pen*. It had the same hospitable point of view as the
American Center itself, and anything that was likely to interest
the membership might be included—from articles of high literary
merit to brisk reports and brisker arguments. The editor, Roger
Dooley, was a volunteer, and so were his assistants. In fact,
there were thirteen committees in existence by 1970, all manned
by hard-working volunteers who were secure in the knowledge
that there would be space at headquarters for whatever was
needed and that they would have the full support of the Executive Secretary.

Another advantage of the long-dreamed-of headquarters was
that it at last made it possible for the American Center to re-
trieve its own history. Its papers had been jumbled into boxes
wherever space could be found, and some of them had become
waterstained or damaged, but now they could be sorted and
placed neatly in their own set of steel files. This was a privilege
shared by very few other Centers, especially the ones in Europe
whose records had been made a deliberate target of destruction
by the Nazis. Moreover, it was a special piece of good fortune
that these records were available to the American Center in time
for the writing of a history in celebration of its fiftieth anniversary—its jubilee year of 1972.

The existence of its own clubhouse made it possible for the
Center to alter some of its traditional patterns of social activity.
The only one that remained unchanged was the giving of the
enormously successful afternoon receptions at the Hotel Pierre.
These still continue and are arranged by the Corresponding
Secretary. Every two weeks during the season, a gathering that
is a glorious mixture of ages, nationalities, costumes and literary

points of view honors the authors of newly published books and
visitors from abroad.

The dinners, however, seemed to have outlived their usefulness. As one member put it, "The cocktail parties provide an
occasion to talk to more people and have a better time, at a
more convenient hour and less expense." The price of the dinners had been rising steadily, and while it had been suggested
many times that it might be possible "to find a quiet room and
have a very simple one-course dinner with wine," no one had
yet found such a place; it would have had to accommodate a
group which might consist of fifty people on one occasion and
a hundred and fifty on another. Therefore, in 1969, all the
dinners were discontinued except for the dinner in May, which
included the business meeting and the annual giving of the prize
for translation.

The dinners were abandoned without regret because they
were no longer needed. The speeches and panels and discussion
groups that they had once accommodated could now be held at
P.E.N. headquarters simply by setting up the folding chairs.
A sideboard held paper cups for the beer and sherry, biscuits
and cookies were always available, and the staff possessed
among its many skills a great gift for affectionate hospitality.

One of the advantages of the new arrangement was that very
little advance preparation was needed. When an African poet
arrived from Biafra, he could be the chief attraction of a poetry
panel assembled on very short notice, or Edward Albee could
be suddenly asked to take part in a panel discussion with a
visiting playwright from Poland. Another advantage was the
lavish wall space in the high-ceilinged room; when Arthur Miller
and his wife, Inge Morath, gave a talk on their trip to Russia,
the walls were hung with enlarged photographs selected from
among those she had taken.

Perhaps, however, the most exhilarating single example of the
kind of expansion that had been made possible by the existence
of a headquarters and a staff was the sudden surge of activity
on the part of the Translation Committee.

During the intervening years this Committee had, as committees frequently will, settled into an orderly but not very

energetic kind of existence. It selected the judges and made the arrangements for the annual Translation Prize, but it initiated very few new projects and its meetings grew increasingly infrequent.

In the spring of 1969, Robert Payne became chairman of the Translation Committee, and the meetings became frequent, energetic and very well attended. Distinguished translators met and argued, sometimes all talking at once in their enthusiasm. By September of 1969, a "Manifesto on Translation" had been drawn up and was ready for distribution at the Menton Congress later in the month. It opened with an eloquent statement on the current lack of respect for translators, those "lost children in the enchanted forest of literature," and it continued with the specific plans that the Committee had already made to do something about this state of affairs.

Chief on its agenda was an ambitious project to bring together some forty translators to participate in the first Conference on the subject ever to be held in the United States. It was going to be a difficult and expensive undertaking, but the "overwhelming desirability of this idea" made the problems seem unimportant. Thirteen thousand dollars was raised—much of it to be spent on airline tickets—and the Conference became the focus of a great deal of excited preparation. The volunteers worked devotedly and so did the staff. Special mention was made of "the extraordinary efforts put forth by our Executive Secretary, Kirsten Michalski, without whom this Conference would not be taking place, and our Corresponding Secretary, Barbara Rice Jones, who has helped her in making efforts far beyond the normal scope of her job."

The Translation Conference was a joy. Twelve of the translators came from abroad, and the rest, many of them foreigners, came from various parts of the United States. Some of them, like the almost legendary Baroness Moura Budberg, had international reputations; some of them worked in special fields and were known to only a few admirers. Each of them had prepared a paper on some special problem in connection with translation, ranging from Gaelic to Yiddish and from "The Tale of Genji" to the poetry of *négritude*. Thirty-nine of these papers were given in five days, with discussions after each one and a whole series of fascinated private conversations. The participants were among their peers, they loved their art, and they gave their delighted best.

There was no sense of nationalism at the Conference. In general, the members of the P.E.N. find it difficult to leave politics behind them, but here they were all citizens of the same country. It appeared for a time that two distinguished Polish translators who had been invited would not be able to attend since they could not get clearance from their government, But, at the last possible moment, the way was opened to them and they were triumphantly present on Monday morning, the 11th of May, 1970, when the opening session convened.

It had been planned to hold two of the afternoon sessions outside P.E.N. headquarters. One was to be at New York University and the other at Columbia University so that the general public could attend. But during this month of May, New York was shaken by a series of student revolts, and at the time when P.E.N. had planned to make use of the colleges they were being occupied illegally by the revolutionary young. The audiences were the losers, but the translators were not. They merely stayed where they were and were given extra cups of coffee by the attentive staff. By this time the P.E.N. headquarters even had a couch, and it helped to provide the easygoing, homelike atmosphere which was one of the factors that made the Conference such a success.*

Just before the Conference was over, the American Center held its annual May dinner, and never had the Translation Prize been given in a more festive atmosphere. All the members of the Conference were guests of honor, and this time the award was not only a check for a thousand dollars but also a gold medal. The winner was Sidney Alexander, who had presented, the previous Monday, a paper on the difficult art of translating from Renaissance Italian.

*The couch was a gift from Franz Schoenberner. He had hoped to be present at the Translation Conference, but he died just before it was held. The Conference was dedicated to his memory and that of two other P.E.N. members—James Putnam and Joseph Barnes—who had served most faithfully a cause in which they all believed.

The following year, the May dinner was again a special occasion for translators. The Conference papers, which had been printed as a book called *The World of Translation,* had only just come off the press. But the printers, carried away by the occasion, managed to bind twenty-five copies and deliver them personally so that they would be available in time for the dinner. Over a hundred dinner guests had gathered at the Hotel Dorset, and they had the first chance to look at the publication. Then copies went out to the contributors, who started, each in his turn, a widening circle. A Bengali poet who wrote in to praise the "beautiful production" and the "flawless printing" of his own paper—"not a single error, down to a comma or a stop"—added that he would like copies for Prime Minister Indira Gandhi, who was deeply interested in literary translation, and for India's ambassador to Poland. *The World of Translation* was in itself an ambassador, and if the Conference had had no other result it would still have been a very great success.

A month after the Translation Conference of 1970, the P.E.N. Congress was held at Seoul. This Congress in South Korea was the first one in Asia since the Tokyo Congress of 1957, and the American delegation included the translator, Donald Keene, who had also attended the Tokyo Congress. The other delegates were well-known fiction writers—John Cheever, Charles Bracelen Flood, John Oliver Killens and John Updike—and Updike gave a formal address. It was one of the advantages of the existence of *The American Pen* that it could print his speech, "Humor in Fiction," and extend the pleasure it had given.

One of the chief topics for discussion at Seoul, as at all P.E.N. Congresses, was that of writers in prison. The American delegation threw particular energy into the case of two Philippine journalists holding Nationalist Chinese passports. Having displeased both governments by their writings, they were deported to Taiwan and imprisoned there. The President of the American Center pointed out that this case opened "a new and frightening vista. . . . To sentence a man in one country for something he has written and published in another, is to maintain that all governments have the right to control the thoughts of their citizens, even when they are thousands of miles away."

It was not easy for the various P.E.N. Centers to uphold "the principles of unhampered transmission" demanded of them by their Charter, and this Congress in Korea took place at a time when a Korean poet was in prison. Before the Congress opened, the members of the Korean Center had protested the imprisonment to their government; they continued to protest it after the Congress was over. "It is thought that their hand was considerably strengthened by the added prestige that the Congress had given to the name of P.E.N. in Korea." In any event, the poet was set free a short time later.

The Writers in Prison Committee of the American Center showed equal energy in protesting cases of injustice in the United States. In May of 1971 the chairman of this Committee, Thomas Fleming, became the new President of the Center, and the outgoing President described its work as "the single most important thing we do." P.E.N. was in a position to protest instantly and consistently any case of the harassment of a writer or the suppression of his writing, and this was an obligation that the American Center had been taking with increasing seriousness. It had, of course, a long root. It was in 1935 that Henry Seidel Canby, as a delegate to the P.E.N. Congress in Barcelona, had drawn attention to the imprisonment of a writer in Haiti and had asked the Congress to protest.

When Charles Flood left office in May of 1971, there was a long list of activities on which to report. There had been a distinguished series of panels on "The Crisis in Criticism," mostly held at P.E.N. headquarters but one of them given at Columbia University so that students could attend. Another P.E.N. series, "The Writer Talks," had been presented on radio, and the whole of it was repeated because of the excellent response. Nor did the Translation Committee have any thought of resting on its laurels; having just seen *The World of Translation* through the press it was now planning a new set of projects.

A great many of these committee activities would have been impossible without the existence of an Executive Secretary, a staff, and a headquarters in which to meet. All the committees, however, were made up entirely of volunteers, just as they had been in the past and as they would continue to be in the future.

These volunteers were men and women heavily involved in their own careers and with very little time to spare. As Flood said in his final speech as President, "Time is the most important thing we all possess." Yet he, like dozens of others, had given lavishly of that irreplaceable commodity. Some members of P.E.N. have taken months or even years out of their lives to do something for the organization that no one else could do as well and that needed to be done. The fact that they considered the time well spent is a sign not only of the excellence of the original idea of the P.E.N. but also of the vigor with which it has grown and flourished.

Many writers feel that any organization, no matter how well intentioned, is somehow suspect. When Henry Miller was asked, in 1957, to join the P.E.N. he wrote back he found it hard to believe that writers would behave better than anyone else; as soon as there was an emergency they promptly forgot their high ideals, their oaths of friendship and their former respect for anyone who now disagreed with them. The President of the American Center replied: "I cannot guarantee that we will remain a virtuous organization in a crisis. I cannot even guarantee that we are a very virtuous one now. But I can say that we try. E.M. Forster once remarked that he would rather be a swimming rat than a sinking ship, which I take to mean that he believes in the principle of energy. Some attempt is better than no attempt at all, and so we can offer you that at least." This was enough for Henry Miller, who promptly joined, and inquired if there was a branch in Iceland. (There was.)

Some writers join the P.E.N., unable to believe that much can be accomplished in international affairs but sure nevertheless that the attempt must be made. As James Baldwin said when he wrote from Corsica to accept membership, it seemed that very little could be done and yet it was necessary to try to do that little.

Sometimes writers would refuse membership in the American Center for the simplest of reasons: they could not afford it. Back in 1936, for instance, John O'Hara did not join because he did not have enough money for dues. "I did not feel that I could afford to pay for my membership." Four years later, however, he wrote P.E.N. to report that he now felt he could manage a check if he were told the amount. Sometimes writers who were already members found themselves in what one of them described as "a state of economic coma," but they did their best to keep up with the dues. Sometimes a writer was trusted for a while and then was able to report a financial triumph. Vilhjalmur Stefansson, for instance, was able to announce that not only had his ship come in but that it was a galleon, and he sent a check for five times the amount that he owed.

Many writers joined P.E.N. without expecting any practical advantages. As Wallace Stevens said when he became a member, it was going to be a "very Platonic" relationship because he could not attend any of the meetings in New York. It was the basic idea that counted—the expression of a principle in which they could all believe—and a translator who was fluent in two dozen languages, from Arabic to Basque and from Sanskrit to Chinese, accepted membership with special enthusiasm. "To tell you a secret, you have fulfilled one of my very private ambitions by your kind act. I have tried my whole life to follow just the ideals expressed in the P.E.N. Charter, to contribute to the free exchange of ideas irrespective of race, nationality or political ideology."

One of the practical advantages of P.E.N. membership is that a letter, signed by the Club Secretary, is available as an introduction to foreign Centers. Back in 1932, when Lewis Mumford asked for a list of his fellow P.E.N. members in Europe, he explained how helpful Alfred Kreymborg had found such a list the preceding year. In 1954, a member who was going abroad admitted to "a certain amount of trepidation. I speak nothing but English and inadequate French. However, the P.E.N. is international!" She returned two months later in a very contented frame of mind. "I visited the P.E.N. in Prague. In fact, they gave quite a reception for me. . . . It was a most extraordinary evening. And in Warsaw and Helsinki as well your introduction bore magnificent fruit."

American members were equally delighted to entertain fellow writers from abroad, and when a questionnaire went out in the spring of 1971 on the subject of offering "home hospitality to foreign writers," there was an enthusiastic response. Offers of dinners and weekends and tours came in from seventeen states, ranging from Maine to Texas and from Missouri to Maryland. "An *excellent* idea," wrote one member approvingly. By now there were over eleven hundred members in the American Center, and most of them knew very well why they belonged.

Sometimes, when a P.E.N. member is in need, the Club can make a practical gesture of affection. A letter from the P.E.N. reached a literary critic while she was in the hospital and she supposed that it was a notification on dues. But instead it was a check, "awarded in recognition of your work." She wrote back that the lift to her spirits meant even more than the money itself, echoing what so many European writers had said when they received food packages after the war. It was again "a present of love," a sign of encouragement and of moral trust.

Checks of this kind are sent to writers whether or not they are members of P.E.N. In one case, a check went to a once-famous writer who was nearly eighty and trying to live on social security. Nine years later, after she had entered a home for the aged, she managed to sell a short story and she sent the money to the American Center along with a letter of gratitude. "God bless P.E.N. for doing so much good."

Usually the check is sent to help in a sudden emergency—an accident or illness. "The haste with which P.E.N. answers such desperate need will never be forgotten by this writer." Once a check went to buy extra time for a biographer who had unexpectedly found new material and knew that the book would take much longer than he had planned. Once it went to buy transportation for a poet who had found work in another city but did not have enough money to get there. Once it went to buy a wheelchair so that a writer could take a job as a teacher, and once it managed not only to pay for a writer's back rent and groceries but "even a new typewriter ribbon." The program is, in fact, a sign of that "comradeship" among writers that Walt Whitman longed for a century ago.

There are no administrative complications. A small committee is given the names of possible recipients from editors, publishers, friends, or from the writers themselves. It then makes a careful, confidential decision, and if the application is approved the money is sent out promptly. The program was begun in 1958 when The New York Community Trust, a foundation for managing charitable funds, asked the American Center to administer the Eleanor Franklin Egan Fund "for the aid of needy American writers." This small fund was later supplemented by a grant from the New Hope Foundation, through the generosity of Lenore Marshall, and the National Council on the Arts now makes a third contribution. For the government has come to realize that good writers are a national resource, like green trees and clear water, and that if they need help they should not go unaided.

The expansion of the work of this particular committee, the enlargement of its sense of responsibility, has been characteristic of a similar enlargement in other areas. For instance, the American Center decided, in 1964, that it needed a precise statement on the subject of censorship, and a committee under the chairmanship of Edgar Johnson drew up a text which was formally approved by the Board.

> In accordance with Article IV of the Charter of the International P.E.N., the American Center affirms its opposition to all censorship of literature, whether of works of imagination, scholarship, information or opinion, whether exercised by official bodies or by private pressure groups or individuals, and whether directed to the prevention of publication or exhibition or to suppression after publication or exhibition.

Six years later, it was clear that this statement had become too limited, since the increasing turbulence of American society had evoked, in response, other forms of suppression. Specifically, the small radical news sheets that had sprung up across the country—the so-called "underground press"—were being subjected to various forms of harassment in an effort to drive them out of existence. Therefore, on the recommendation of the Censorship Committee and the Writers in Prison Committee, the Board voted in October of 1970 to enlarge the area of responsibility. "For the protection of free speech and literary expression, protests against forms of suppression of the media of such speech and expression fall within the limits of matter on which the American Center may take public positions."

The ability to respond to new conditions is one of the characteristics of growth, and a striking example of this was the Dublin Congress of 1971 in which P.E.N. celebrated its fiftieth year. From the literary point of view it was not a remarkable Congress, although the Irish were\charming hosts and a variety of papers were read. What made this jubilee Congress of special interest was the contrasting point of view of the two International Presidents. They were good friends and good writers, but their speeches could not have been more unlike. The outgoing President looked backward, as a philosopher; the incoming President looked forward, as a man of action. Between them they managed, in that jubilee year, to symbolize the basic realities of P.E.N.

The outgoing President was Pierre Emmanuel of the French Center—poet, member of the French Academy, child of the old European humanism. He called the continued existence of P.E.N. "a miracle of precariousness," and used the occasion of its fiftieth anniversary as a time for taking stock.

> When a man or an organization is closely linked to history and when the history is that of a century as tragic and enigmatic as ours, it is natural and doubtless necessary that they should become aware of their fatigue and their signs of wear and tear, if only in order to measure the effort required to stay alive. To stay alive, not to outlive themselves. For many men and organizations manage, by hook or by crook, to survive beyond their reason for being. They have not known how . . . to keep faith with their original idea through the ambiguity and destructiveness of an epoch which no ivory tower can stand up against, no mind or spirit can claim to escape. *

When P.E.N. was born in 1921, "European literature and thought still dominated the world's intellectual life," but this era died in the year that Hitler ordered the Burning of the Books. "The year 1933 marked the end of European supremacy and perhaps also of European civilization . . . the end of one world, but not yet the beginning of another." What seemed chiefly to survive was

*This speech was given in French. The translation is by Frances Frenaye.

the continued threat of political oppression, reinforced by the huge, mindless strides of postwar technology.

It was indeed the end of a world when a man like Emmanuel could say that he no longer believed in the authority of European civilization. "It is not that I have lost confidence in the workings of the European conscience but that I no longer believe the most 'highly developed' nations have the prerogative of teaching others. . . . Whatever be the present situation of the weak, whether they are free or oppressed, the shape of the future world depends on their awareness of their cultural identity and the energy that they put into preserving it."

This abnegation of the traditional role of the West, this retreat from the old theory of dominance, gave Emmanuel's speech a kind of autumnal quality. He could see changes coming, in P.E.N. as well as everywhere else, but he welcomed them in his own way, as a philosopher. "My P.E.N. experience tells me that P.E.N. is not a comfortable meeting-place and that it is better that your comfort should be disturbed by important questions than by petty ones. When it comes down to it, there is little comfort in either intelligence or imagination, and yet P.E.N. needs both of these in order to endure in the universe that we see developing around us."

These qualities of intelligence and imagination were fortunately very well exemplified by the incoming International President of P.E.N. This was Heinrich Böll of the West German Center, whose energy was matched by his dislike of arrogance in any form. In his speech he welcomed the "nations coming into history now" after having been for so long treated with contempt by the dominant West, and he went further than that. "There are also the nations within the traditional nations—the underprivileged, the homeless, the stranded ones, the frustrated in over-industrialized society. These nations within nations no longer wish to be just the subject of literature, that is to say, subjected to literature. They require their own expression, they create their own language." The West German Center had, in fact, already set up a relationship with factory workers, whose ways of expressing themselves turned out to be more original and more effective than the diction of the owners of the factories. It was this same sense of hospitality that had made the American Center set up a relationship with young drug addicts from the ghetto and publish some of their work in *The American Pen.*

When Böll turned to the subject of the ceaseless struggle to get writers out of prison, he could only counsel the P.E.N. never to lose heart. "It is mainly a question of finding the right moment, and if every sixth or seventh resolution, carefully timed and delivered, saves somebody from a few months of prison—everyone who ever was imprisoned will know what that means. I do not just guess; I know. People were saved by resolutions, not only from prison but even from death sentences." One of the most constructive acts of the past year had been the establishment by the Dutch Center of an emergency fund to be used both for the families of writers in prison and for the writers themselves if censorship had taken away their livelihood. Individuals and Centers make donations to this fund, and the Dutch Center has made itself responsible for the difficult and sometimes dangerous task of distributing the money.

The New York Times published a report on the Dublin Congress which described the P.E.N. as a kind of a "joke" in literary circles. Curiously enough, Pierre Emmanuel mentioned this point himself when he spoke of the Charter. "P.E.N.'s charter is made up of big words. . . . They strengthen you in exact proportion to your faith in them. And since things are as they are, let us admit that this faith has something laughable about it. Everything leagues together to prevent it from working, and intellectuals are not the last to contribute to its demolition." Emmanuel did not fear for the Charter; he feared only that P.E.N. would forget to take it seriously. Nor did he see any merit in the proliferation of new Centers unless there was a corresponding expansion of the imagination. "Is P.E.N.'s missionary spirit, which every year carries its charter like the ark of the covenant to a different part of the world, attached to the memory of a past era?" Emmanuel hoped it was not; Böll was sure it was not. Between them, they celebrated both P.E.N.'s past and its future in the jubilee Congress that was held at Dublin in 1971.

P.E.N. was born in optimism, and it is from the optimists that it continues to derive its support. They exemplify what Emmanuel called "the miraculous conviction of all the members that they are, each one in his place and as best he can, witnesses and servants of a truth, simple in their eyes, expressed by mankind's most meaningful words: freedom, peace, understanding, mutual respect, humanity." That was the way P.E.N. began, half a century ago and in a very different world. That is the way it will continue, servant of a truth that does not desert its servants. Hitler expected his Third Reich to last for a millennium; it is now dust. The P.E.N., which had nothing to oppose to the power of the sword except the power of the word, is still most cheerfully alive. Its next fifty years will be even better than its past fifty if it continues to remember from what it derives its strength.

Appendix

List of Presidents of the American Center

1922-23	Booth Tarkington
1923-24	Booth Tarkington
1924-25	Carl Van Doren
1925-26	Carl Van Doren
1926-27	Henry Seidel Canby
1927-28	Henry Seidel Canby – Will Irwin
1928-29	Will Irwin
1929-30	Will Irwin
1930-31	Will Irwin – Carl Van Doren
1931-32	Carl Van Doren – Robert Frost
1932-33	Robert Frost
1933-34	Robert Frost
1934-35	Robert Frost
1935-36	Robert Frost – Dorothy Thompson
1936-37	Dorothy Thompson
1937-38	Dorothy Thompson
1938-39	Dorothy Thompson
1939-40	Dorothy Thompson – Robert Nathan
1940-41	Robert Nathan
1941-42	Robert Nathan
1942-43	Robert Nathan – Carl Carmer
1943-44	Carl Carmer
1944-45	Carl Carmer

1945-46 Carl Carmer
1946-47 Carl Carmer — John Mason Brown
1947-48 John Mason Brown — Henry Seidel Canby
1948-49 Henry Seidel Canby — Henry Steele Commager
1949-50 Henry Steele Commager
1950-51 Henry Steele Commager — John Farrar
1951-52 John Farrar
1952-53 John Farrar
1953-54 John Farrar — James Thomas Flexner
1954-55 James Thomas Flexner — Marchette Chute
1955-56 Marchette Chute
1956-57 Marchette Chute — Leon Edel
1957-58 Leon Edel
1958-59 Leon Edel — B. J. Chute
1959-60 B. J. Chute
1960-61 B. J. Chute — Edgar Johnson
1961-62 Edgar Johnson
1962-63 Edgar Johnson - John Farrar
1963-64 John Farrar
1964-65 John Farrar — Lewis Galantière
1965-66 Lewis Galantière
1966-67 Lewis Galantière — Robert Halsband
1967-68 Robert Halsband
1968-69 Robert Halsband — Charles Bracelen Flood
1969-70 Charles Bracelen Flood
1970-71 Charles Bracelen Flood — Thomas Fleming
1971-72 Thomas Fleming

List of International P.E.N. Congresses

1923	London	1948	Copenhagen
1924	New York	1949	Venice
1925	Paris	1950	Edinburgh
1926	Berlin	1951	Lausanne
1927	Brussels	1952	Nice
1928	Oslo	1953	Dublin
1929	Vienna	1954	Amsterdam
1930	Warsaw	1955	Vienna
1931	Amsterdam	1956	London
1932	Budapest	1957	Tokyo
1933	Dubrovnik	1959	Frankfurt
1934	Edinburgh	1960	Rio de Janeiro
1935	Barcelona	1964	Oslo
1936	Buenos Aires	1965	Bled
1937	Paris	1966	New York
1938	Prague	1967	Abidjan
1941	London	1969	Menton
1946	Stockholm	1970	Seoul
1947	Zurich	1971	Dublin

Text of P.E.N. Charter

International P.E.N. affirms that:

1. Literature, national though it be in origin, knows no frontiers, and should remain common currency between nations in spite of political or international upheavals.

2. In all circumstances, and particularly in time of war, works of art, the patrimony of humanity at large, should be left untouched by national or political passion.

3. Members of the P.E.N. should at all times use what influence they have in favour of good understanding and mutual respect between nations; they pledge themselves to do their utmost to dispel race, class and national hatreds and to champion the ideal of one humanity living in peace in one world.

4. The P.E.N. stands for the principle of unhampered transmission of thought within each nation and between all nations, and members pledge themselves to oppose any form of suppression of freedom of expression in the country and community to which they belong. The P.E.N. declares for a free press and opposes arbitrary censorship in time of peace. It believes that the necessary advance of the world towards a more highly organized political and economic order renders a free criticism of governments, administrations and institutions imperative. And since freedom implies voluntary restraint, members pledge themselves to oppose such evils of a free press as mendacious publication, deliberate falsehood and distortion of facts for political and personal ends.

Membership in P.E.N. is open to all qualified writers, editors and translators who subscribe to these aims, without regard to nationality, race, colour or religion.

Index

Abe Lincoln in Illinois, 25
Abidjan Congress, *see* Congresses
Adler, Stella, 55
Africa, 12, 80, 84
Albee, Edward, 82, 91
Alexander, Sidney, 93
Aley, Maxwell, 5
Algonquin Hotel, 21, 22, 56
Ambassador Hotel, 35, 36, 56
America-Italy Society, 58
American Academy of Arts and
    Letters, 83
American Center
    founding, 5-6, 28, 51
    emblem, 47-48
    bylaws, 58, 62
    tax exemption, 45-46, 62, 63
    questionnaires, 33-34, 36, 97-98
    relief packages, 39-41, 44, 45, 66,
        98
    Congresses
        of 1924, 7-8, 9, 12, 43, 49, 51,
            76
        during World's Fair, 22-28, 29,
            31, 32, 45, 50

    attempted, 43, 44-45, 46, 47
    of 1966, 76, 78-84, 86, 87
    publications
        histories of Center, 37-38, 41-
            42, 44, 90
        P.E.N. News, 59
        "Proceedings of the XXXIV
            International P.E.N. Congress,"
            82
        lists of grants and awards, 89
        The American Pen, 90, 94, 102
        "Manifesto on Translation," 92
        The World of Translation, 94, 95
    government support, *see* National
        Council on the Arts
American Civil Liberties Union, 69
American Heritage, 58
American Pen, The, see American
    Center, publications
Amsterdam, 14
Amsterdam Congresses, *see* Con-
    gresses
Anderson, Robert, 60
Anthony, Joseph, 5, 15
Arendt, Hannah, 85

Areopagitica, 16, 31, 76
Argentina, 83
Argentine Center, 74, 80
Asch, Sholem, 14
Asia Foundation, 63
Atherton, Gertrude, 9
Auden, W. H., 59
Austin, Mary, 7
Australia, 14
Austria, 30
Austrian Center, 13, 30, 34, 65
Authors League, 69

Baldwin, James, 96
Baraka, Imamu Amiri, *see* Jones,
  LeRoi
Barcelona Congress, *see* Congresses
Barnes, Joseph, 93*fn.*
Barnouw, Dr., 8
Barreda, Octavio, 7-8
Baruch, Bernard, 32
Beatty, Bessie, 22, 23, 24, 25, 29,
  32, 33, 34-35, 37, 38, 44-45, 60
Beautiful Joe, 20
Belgian Center, 12, 44
Belgium, 7, 30
Belloc, Hilaire, 21
Bellow, Saul, 81
Benchley, Robert, 6
Benes, Eduard, 27
Benét, Stephen, 34
Bennett, Arnold, 4
Berlin Congress, *see* Congresses
Best, Marshall, 87
Biafra, 91
Bibo, Istvan, 68
Black, Alexander, 5, 6, 7, 12-13
Bled Congress, *see* Congresses
Bogan, Louise, 59, 60
Böll, Heinrich, 101-102
Book-of-the-Month Club, 45, 74
Bookman, The, 5, 51
Borgese, G. A., 26
Brazil, 83

Brazil Center, 80
Breit, Harvey, 59
Brevoort Hotel, 20, 21
Brighton, 68
Brown, John Mason, 108
Brussels, 59
Brussels Congress, *see* Congresses
Budapest, 15, 67, 68
Budapest Congress, *see* Congresses
Budberg, Moura, 92
Buenos Aires Congress, *see* Con-
  gresses
Bulgaria, 33
Burnett, Frances Hodgson, 6
"Burning of the Books," 15-16, 18,
  34, 100
bylaws, *see* American Center

C.I.A., *see* Central Intelligence
  Agency
Caillois, Roger, 80
Camus, Albert, 68
Canada, 14
Canby, Henry Seidel, 9, 10, 11, 12,
  16, 17, 18, 23, 35, 36, 39, 48, 50,
  69, 95, 107, 108; Canby resolution,
  11, 16, 17, 18, 42, 42*fn.*
Capek, Karel, 14
CARE, 40
Carmer, Carl, 107-108
Carnegie Endowment International
  Center, 71
Carnegie Endowment for Inter-
  national Peace, 10
Carver, David, 61
Case, Frank, 22
Castro, Amerijo, 8
Cather, Willa, 5
Catton, Bruce, 58
Cenedella, Betsy, 86-87, 88
censorship, 16, 42*fn.,* 43-44, 46,
  94, 99, 102
Center for Writers in Exile, 66
Centers, *see individual listings*

Central America, 80, 82
Central Intelligence Agency (C.I.A.),
   75, 76
Century Company, 5
Charter, 46, 69, 72, 77, 86, 95, 97,
   99, 102; formation, 12, 14, 16,
   42, 42*fn.*, 43-44; full text, 110
Cheever, John, 94
Chekhova, Mme., 8
Chesterton, G. K., 4
Chile, 27, 81, 83
Chilean Center, 80
China, 14; Nationalist China, 94
Chute, B.J., 82, 108
Chute, Marchette, 108
Coffee House Club, 6, 51
Colombia, 27
Columbia Institute of Arts and
   Sciences, 60
Columbia University, 93, 95
Commager, Henry Steele, 61, 108
Commodore Hotel, 20
Congresses
   Abidjan (1967), 84-85
   Amsterdam (1931), 14; (1954),
      58, 61, 73*fn.*
   Barcelona (1935), 95
   Berlin (1926), 11-12, 14
   Bled (1965), 76, 77, 78, 79, 81-82
   Budapest (1932), 14-15, 18
   Buenos Aires (1936), 23
   Brussels (1927), 10, 12, 14, 16,
      42*fn.*, 46
   Copenhagen (1948), 46-47
   Dublin (1953), 61; (1971), 100,
      102
   Dubrovnik (1933), 11, 15,
      16-18, 26, 27, 42*fn.*, 46,
      66, 76
   Edinburgh (1934), 42*fn.*; (1950),
      49
   Frankfurt (1959), 67
   Lausanne (1951), 54
   London (1923), 7; (1941), 30-31,
      37; (1956), 61-62

   Menton (1969), 92
   New York (1924 and 1966), *see*
      American Center, Congresses
   Nice (1952), 61
   Oslo (1928), 12, 43; (1964), 80
   Paris (1925), 9-10; (1937), 23
   Prague (1938), 27
   Rio de Janeiro (1960), 68-69
   Seoul (1970), 94-95
   Stockholm (1946), 42-44
   Tokyo (1957), 62-63, 64-65, 66,
      67, 70, 71-72, 78, 94
   Venice (1949), 48, 49
   Vienna (1955), 61
   Warsaw (1930), 13
   Zurich (1947), 44, 45
   For complete list, see page 109
Connelly, Marc, 6, 43, 60
Conrad, Joseph, 4
Copenhagen Congress, *see* Con-
   gresses
Cousins, Norman, 36
Cracow University, 39
Cuban Center, 78-79
Czechoslovakia, 7, 27, 30, 79, 85

Dachau, 34
Daniel, Yuli, 85
Danish Center, 13, 46
Dashiell, Alfred, 16
Davila, Carlos, 27
Dawson Scott, Mrs. C. A., 3-4, 5,
   8-9, 10, 18, 88
Declaration of Independence, 27, 78
Dell, Floyd, 7
Denmark, 7, 8, 30
Dery, Tibor, 66, 67-68, 72
Dewey, John, 20
Dooley, Roger, 90
Dorset Hotel, 94
Dos Passos, John, 37, 48-49, 63, 64
Dublin Congresses, *see* Congresses
Dubrovnik, 11
Dubrovnik Congress, *see* Congresses
Duhamel, Georges, 38

Dutch Center, 102
Dutton & Co., E. P., 10

Edel, Leon, 82, 108
Edinburgh Congresses, *see*
    Congresses
Egan Fund, 99
Eisenhower, Dwight D., 61, 65
Eliot, T. S., 53*fn.*, 68
Ellison, Ralph, 61, 74, 82
emblem, *see* American Center
Emmanuel, Pierre, 100-101, 102,
    103
English Center, 12, 14, 30, 31, 34,
    35, 39, 43, 88
Estonian Center, 49

Farfield Foundation, 58, 61, 63, 65,
    69, 75, 76
Farrar, John, 5-6, 51-53, 58, 108
Farrell, James, 61
Field, Marshall, 32
Finland, 42
Fleming, Thomas, 95, 108
Flexner, James Thomas, 58, 108
Flood, Charles Bracelen, 89, 94, 95,
    96, 108
Florence Restaurant, 4
Ford, Ford Madox, 20
Ford Foundation, 81
Forster, E. M., 29, 31, 66, 76-77, 96
France, 7, 20, 30
France, Anatole, 5
Frankfurt Congress, *see*
    Congresses
Frenaye, Frances, 100*fn.*
French Academy, 40*fn.*, 100
French Center, 5, 8, 12, 23, 34, 38,
    44, 100
Frost, Robert, 6, 23-24, 53, 74, 107
Fuentes, Carlos, 86

Galantière, Lewis, 75, 78, 79, 80,
    87, 108

Galsworthy, John, 3-4, 5, 6-7, 8, 10,
    11, 12, 14, 15, 19, 31, 66
Gandhi, Indira, 94
General Motors, 25, 27-28
Geneva, 10
German Center, 12, 16, 17, 18, 46;
    East German, 79;
    West German, 101
Germany, 10, 15, 19, 20, 27, 33
Gestapo, 38
Ghana, 80
Gide, André, 11
Ginsberg, Allen, 85
Glasgow, Ellen, 6
Goebbels, Joseph, 26
grants and awards, lists of, *see*
    American Center, publications
Grass, Günter, 57
Greece, 40, 85
Greenwich Village, 81
Guildhall, 61

Haiti, 85, 95
Halsband, Robert, 108
Hammerstein, Oscar, 55
Harcourt, Alfred, 20
Harkness Theatre, 55
Hay, Julius, 66, 67-68. 72
Hays, Arthur Garfield, 36
Heckscher, August, 74
Helsinki, 97
Hersey, John, 63, 64, 82
Hess, Myra, 4
Hitler, Adolf, 15, 16, 18, 27, 29,
    32, 100, 103
Hoffman, Daniel, 59
Holland, 30
Horthy, Admiral, 15, 18
Howard, Sidney, 6
Hudson, Jane, 35, 36, 43, 49, 50,
    53*fn.*, 69
Huebsch, Ben, 39-40, 44
Hughes, Langston, 60, 71, 74
Hungarian Academy of Sciences, 65

Hungarian Center, 65, 66, 68;
  debate over, 65, 66, 67
Hungary, 40, 65, 68

Iceland Center, 96
Immigration Department, 86
India, 14, 20, 94
Institute of International Education,
  81, 88
Internal Revenue Office, 45, 46
International Institute of Ibero-
  American Literature, 71
International P.E.N., *see* P.E.N.,
  International
Irwin, Will, 13, 16, 18, 20, 36, 41,
  107
Isaacs, Julius, 62, 78, 87
Italian Center, 30
Italy, 7, 30
Ivory Coast Center, 80, 84

Jamaica Center, 74
Jameson, Storm, 30, 39, 53*fn.*
Janeway, Elizabeth, 59, 63, 82
Japan, 14, 63
Japanese Center, 46, 63, 70, 71
Jaspers, Karl, 68
Johnson, Edgar, 99, 108
Jones, Barbara Rice, *see* Rice,
  Barbara
Jones, LeRoi (Imamu Amiri Baraka),
  74, 74*fn.*, 85-86
Justice Department, 82

Kastner, Erich, 68
Kawabata, Yasunari, 71-72
Keene, Donald, 63, 64, 70, 94
Kennedy, John F., 74, 79
Kenneth, Claire, 65-66
Kenya, 80
Killens, John Oliver, 94
Kleeman, Rita Halle, 34, 49
Koestler, Arthur, 38
Komroff, Manuel, 40

Korea, South, 94, 95
Korean Center, 95
Kreymborg, Alfred, 97

Lausanne Congress, *see*
  Congresses
Lawrence, D. H., 5
Laxness, Halldor, 14
Leach, Henry Goddard, 12, 22, 43
League of International Coopera-
  tion, 10
League of Nations, 11, 33
Leaves of Grass, 25
Lehmann, John, 61
Lemay, Harding, 60
Lewis, Sinclair, 20-21
Leyden, University of, 73*fn.*
Lippmann, Walter, 6
London, 4, 18, 30, 42, 62, 76
London Congresses, *see* Congresses
Loos, Anita, 55
Lotos Club, 54, 54*fn.,* 55

Macrae, John, 10
Mailer, Norman, 58, 59
Maison Internationale, 38
"Manifesto on Translation," *see*
  American Center, publications
Mann, Klaus, 49
Mann, Thomas, 12, 26, 27, 32, 41
Marquis, Don, 20
Marshall, Lenore, 82, 99
Masefield, John, 4, 19
Masque of Reason, 53
Maugham, Somerset, 39
Mauriac, François, 68
McGinley, Phyllis, 60
Melcher, Daniel, 87
Melcher, Frederic, 24, 45, 49-50, 87
Menton Congress, *see* Congresses
Membré, Henri, 38
Mexico, 8, 80, 83
Michalski, Kirsten, 88, 92
Mihajlov, Mihajlo, 76, 78

Miller, Arthur, 55, 77, 79, 83, 91
Miller, Henry, 96
Milton, John, 16, 31
Moore, Marianne, 59
Morath, Inge, 91
Moravia, Alberto, 58-59, 68
Morgenthau, Henry, 32
Morrow, William, 10
Mumford, Lewis, 20, 97
Museum of Modern Art, 83

Nathan, Robert, 16, 107
National Book Awards, 56
National Council on the Arts, 81, 87, 99
National Institute of Arts and Letters, 83
Nazism, 15-16, 17, 26, 34, 35, 48, 54, 76, 90
Neruda, Pablo, 81-82
Netherlands, the, 8
Nevins, Allan, 58
New Hope Foundation, 99
New Weston Hotel, 52, 56, 71
New York Community Trust, The, 99
New York Congresses, *see* American Center, Congresses
New York Public Library, The, 48
New York Times, The, 47, 75, 83, 102
New York University, 60, 81, 93
Nice Congress, *see* Congresses
Nigeria, 80
Nobel Prize, 15, 20, 71
Norris, Kathleen, 6
Norway, 7, 30

O'Casey, Sean, 26, 28, 31
Offit, Sidney, 89
O'Hara, John, 59, 96-97
O'Neill, Eugene, 6
Oslo Congresses, *see* Congresses
Ott, Olga, 8

Ould, Hermon, 10, 13-14, 19, 23, 26, 29-30, 31, 32, 35, 36, 38, 39, 42-43, 46, 47, 50, 51, 54, 61
Overseas Press Club, 74

Parandowski, Jan, 48
Paris, 10, 30, 38
Paris Congresses, *see* Congresses
Park-Sheraton Hotel, 58
Payne, Robert, 92
"P.E.N. in the City," 89-90, 102
P.E.N., International
  founding, 3-4
  first meeting, 4, 14
  meaning of initials, 4
  Executive Committee, 18-19, 37, 47, 48, 57, 68, 69, 73
  for charter, see Charter
  for Congresses, see Congresses
  for Centers, see individual listings
P.E.N. News, see American Center, publications
Pennsylvania Hotel, 7
Peru, 80, 83
Philippines, 94
Pick, Robert, 40
Pierre Hotel, 56-57, 74, 90
Plaza Hotel, 25, 83
Poland, 13, 30, 39, 70, 91, 93, 94
Polish Center, 13, 48, 70
Porter, Katherine Anne, 59
Portugal, 85
Prague, 27, 97
Prague Congress, *see* Congresses
"Proceedings of the XXXIV International P.E.N. Congress," *see* American Center, publications
Publishers' Weekly, 87
Purdy, Theodore, 70, 72
Putnam, Arthur James, 60-61, 64, 66, 82, 87, 93*fn.*

Radio Free Europe, 72
Raymond resolution, 42, 42*fn.*

Reichstag, 15
relief packages, *see* American Center
Rice, Barbara (Barbara Rice Jones), 88, 92
Rice, Elmer, 44, 60, 61, 63, 69, 73-74, 82, 88
Rio de Janeiro Congress, *see* Congresses
Robinson, Edwin Arlington, 6
Rockefeller Center, 55
Rolland, Romain, 11
Rolo, Charles, 59
Romains, Jules, 8, 13, 27
Rome, 30, 61, 73
Roosevelt, Eleanor, 22, 25, 53
Roosevelt, Franklin D., 25
Rumania, 7
Russia, 8, 19, 91
Russian writers, 13, 19, 57, 72, 77, 79, 85

Salisbury, Harrison, 72
San Francisco branch, 9
Saturday Review of Literature, 36
Scherman, Harry, 74-75
Schoenberner, Franz, 54, 54*fn.*, 93*fn.*
Senegal Center, 80
Seoul Congress, *see* Congresses
Shaw, George Bernard, 4
Sherry-Netherland Hotel, 56
Sherwood, Robert, 25, 53
Silone, Ignazio, 68, 74, 84
Simenon, Georges, 58
Simplicissimus, 54
Simpson, Louis, 59
Sinyavsky, Andrei, 85
Sitwell, Osbert, 20
Slovene Center, 76, 78
South America, 14, 27, 56, 69, 80, 82
Soviet Writers Congress, 19
Spain, 7, 8, 27, 85
State Department, 57, 62, 79, 82, 86

Stefansson, Vilhjalmur, 97
Stegner, Wallace, 69
Steinbeck, John, 63-64, 78
Stevens, Wallace, 97
Stockholm, 23, 29, 42
Stockholm Congress, *see* Congresses
Styron, William, 55, 59
Sweden, 7, 43
Swedish Center, 23, 43

Tagore, Rabindranath, 20
Taiwan, 94
Tarkington, Booth, 6, 7, 20, 107
tax exemption, *see* American Center
Thompson, Dorothy, 20, 23, 24, 107
Time, 27
Times, London, 62
Tokyo, 64
Tokyo Congress, *see* Congresses
Toller, Ernst, 17-18, 26, 27
Town Hall Club, 55, 58
translation, 9-11, 64, 69-71, 72, 74-75, 91-94, 95, 97
translation conferences
  Warsaw (1958), 69, 70
  New York (1970), 92-93, 93*fn.*, 94
Translation Prize, 74-75, 91, 92, 93
Treasury Department, 62

UNESCO, 70, 80
United Nations, 44, 68, 71, 81, 82, 83
Updike, John, 94
Uruguay, 83
Uruguay Center, 80

Valéry, Paul, 38
Van Doren, Carl, 5, 7, 9, 107
Venezuela, 80, 83
Venice Congress, *see* Congresses
Vercours, 38
Vidal, Gore, 55

Vienna, 40, 65
Vienna Congress, *see* Congresses
Vietnam, South, 85
Vining, Elizabeth Gray, 63

Waldorf Astoria Hotel, 45, 56
Walpole, Hugh, 20
Warren, Robert Penn, 59
Warsaw, 69, 70, 97
Warsaw Congress, *see* Congresses
Washington, D.C., 25, 45
Washington Square, 60, 81
Wedgwood, C. V., 58, 61
Wells, H. G., 15, 17, 19, 29
Werfel, Franz, 30
Wescott, Glenway, 59, 82
White, Walter, 37
Whitman, Walt, 3, 25, 98
Wiggin, Kate Douglas, 5
Wilder, Thornton, 20, 37, 85
Wilhelm, Prince, 43, 47

Williams, Jesse Lynch, 5
Wodehouse, P. G., 21, 85
Wolfe, Thomas, 81
World of Translation, The, see
     American Center, publications
World's Fair, 22-23, 24, 25
World's Fair Congress, *see* Amer-
     ican Center, Congresses
writers in need, funds for, 98-99
writers in prison, 14, 66, 67-69, 76,
     84-85, 94, 95, 102; action by
     American Center, 67-68, 72, 85-
     86, 94, 95
Writers' War Board, 34, 35
Wylie, Elinor, 6

Yugoslavia, 11, 76, 78

Zurich Congress, *see* Congresses
Zweig, Stefan, 29